Happy Colors!
Cozy Baker

KALEIDOSCOPES

Wonders Of Wonder

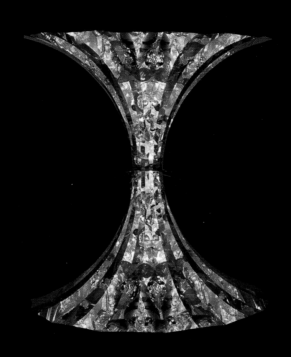

COZY BAKER

Copyright © 1999 by Cozy Baker

Developmental Editor: Cyndy Lyle Rymer

Technical Editor: Sara Kate MacFarland

Copy Editor: Vera Tobin

Book Design: Lesley Gasparetti

Book Production: Kathy Lee

Cover Design: Christina Jarumay

Illustrator: Jay Richards

Front Cover Photographs: Top Row–Charles Karadimos (left); Randy & Shelley Knapp (center and right). Middle Row–Tom & Sherry Rupert (far left); Luc & Sallie Durette (left); Van Cort Instruments (scope); Randy & Shelley Knapp (far right). Bottom Row–David Sugich (left); Luc & Sallie Durette (center and right); Marc Tickle (front and back cover flaps).

Title page image from "Crystal Rapture" by Bob & Grace Ade

Each chapter opening image and photograph by Adam Peiperl; images on pages 7, 19, 33, and 121 by Randy & Shelley Knapp; pages 65 and 103 by Luc & Sallie Durette; page 47 by Sherry Moser; page 89 and back cover by Marc Tickle; page 58 "Iridescent Dreams," and page 60 "Ann" by Joel Silverman; page 99 composite of two photos of images from "Fibonacci" by John Flowerdew; page 108 "Mailbox" by Tom Chouteau; photos of Durettes' interiors on pages 71 and 129 by Doug Buxton; all other photos of Durettes' work by Thomas Ferguson.

Text photos are courtesy of the author or individual artist unless otherwise specified.

Library of Congress Cataloging-in-Publication Data

Baker, Cozy

    Kaleidoscopes : wonders of wonder / Cozy Baker

        p.   cm.

    Includes bibliographical references and index.

    ISBN 1-57120-063-0

    1. Kaleidoscopes.   I. Title.

    QC373.K3B347 1999

    688.7'2—dc21   98-37213

                                  CIP

Published by C&T Publishing, Inc.

P.O. Box 1456

Lafayette, California 94549

Printed in Hong Kong

10   9   8   7   6   5   4   3   2

CONTENTS

Dedicated to the cherished memory of my beloved son Randall, whose untimely death at the age of 23 led me on a search for beauty in the midst of tragedy. It was during this search in 1982 that I discovered not only the beauty, but the healing value of the kaleidoscope.

"Jubilation Star" image
by David Sugich

Image and photo by Adam Peiperl

In the midst of quietness

with no thought of what was

or what will be

a tantalizing glimpse of beauty

then another

. . . and yet another

For those who glance quickly

there is pleasure

for those who take time to gaze

there is peace and tranquility

for all who fall under its spell

there is joy and there is ecstasy

PREFACE

The kaleidoscope's fascination is timeless and its intrigue is universal. The very word recaptures childhood enchantment and promises magic. Surely no other device offers such a complete spectrum of delight. I count among my many blessings all the colors, splendors, and wonders of the kaleidoscope.

KALEIDOSCOPES: ORIGIN AND HISTORY

The kaleidoscope is as symbolic of peace and harmony • as a dove carrying an olive branch or children from all nations holding hands

Reflective symmetry has been observed since ancient times. Legend claims that early Egyptians would place two or three slabs of highly polished limestone together at different angles and watch with fascination as mandalas were formed by human dancers. It was not until centuries later, however, that this optical phenomenon was encased in one small tube and given a name. The kaleidoscope was invented in 1816 by Sir David Brewster. He was a man with as many facets as his invention. Whether delving into scientific research, religion, philosophy, education, optics, photography, writing, inventions, or life on other planets, Sir David pursued each endeavor with incredible energy.

David Brewster was born in Jedburgh, an obscure country town in the midst of the Scottish lowlands, on December 11, 1781. He was recognized as a child prodigy, and constructed a telescope when only ten years old. This would prove indicative of the chief bent of Brewster's work and genius. Nature

Opposite: Portrait of Sir David Brewster reproduced by permission of the Royal Society of Edinburgh

endowed him with some of its choice gifts: close observation, unceasing inquiry, and a scientific proclivity. Far before his peers, he absorbed all that was available in elementary Scottish education. Because he evidenced an exceptional aptitude for learning, his family decided that he should study for the ministry of the Church of Scotland. Thus, at the tender age of 12, he was consigned to the University of Edinburgh, where he continued his intellectual achievements. He was greatly admired at the university for his unusual academic ability, and was generously welcomed into the intimate fellowship of the distinguished professors of philosophy and mathematics. The zenith of his formal education was reached at age 19 when he was awarded an honorary master of arts degree. This carried with it a license to preach the gospel as a minister of the Scottish Established Church.

Of Brewster's brief pulpit episode, James Hogg, a colleague, wrote in a letter to publisher James Fraser: " . . . he was licensed, but the first day he mounted the pulpit was the last, for he had then, if he has not still, a nervous something about him that made him swither when he heard his own voice and saw a congregation eyeing him; so he sticked his discourse, and vowed never to try that job again. It was a pity for Kirk, (the National Church of Scotland) . . . but it was a good day for Science . . . for if the doctor had gotten a manse, he might most likely have taken to his toddy like other folk."

Original books by Brewster, German kaleidoscope, lenticular stereoscope, kaleidoscope teaching tool. Photo by John Woodin

This was in the year 1801, and Brewster immediately turned his great talents to two of his life-long interests, the study of optics and the development of scientific instruments. For twelve years he conducted a series of experiments that were revealed to the public in *A Treatise Upon New Philosophical Instruments*, published in 1813.

Brewster's treatise did not represent his only accomplishments during this period. In 1807, at the age of 26, the University of Aberdeen awarded him a Doctor of Letters degree, the highest literary distinction of that era and a truly unique achievement for one of his age. But this was not all—in 1808, he was elected a Fellow of the Royal Society of Edinburgh, and the same year became editor of the *Edinburgh Encyclopedia*, a position he distinguished with excellence for more than 20 years.

In 1810, Brewster married Juliet McPherson. Their marriage, which produced four sons and one daughter, was apparently a happy one, lasting forty years until Juliet's death. It was not until a few months before Brewster's seventy-fifth birthday that he married his second wife, Jane Purnell. As well as being a devoted companion, she presented him with a daughter who became the bright light of his golden years. Very little else is recorded about Brewster's family life. It might be noted, however, that Sir D.B., as he was called by his friends, paid little attention, if any, to genealogy, except for the suggestion that one of his ancestors, William Elder Brewster, led the noble band of English dissenters to America on the Mayflower in 1610.

Shortly after Brewster's death, his daughter, Mrs. Margaret M. Gordon, published a biography entitled *The Home Life of Sir David Brewster*. The word "home" was loosely interpreted, and throughout 500 pages Mrs. Gordon cites Brewster's many activities, including the publication of over 2,000 scientific papers. Surprisingly candid in some of her observations, she did not conceal the fact that her distinguished father could be "irritable, impatient, litigious, and verbally aggressive," hastening to explain on the other hand that "he was a man with a strong personality, strong constitution and possessed a great personal charm when he chose to exercise it."

It was in 1811, while writing an article on "Burning Instruments," Brewster investigated Buffon's Needle theory (considered to be the first problem in geometric probability). Brewster did not consider Buffon's proposal practical. However, it sparked an idea that produced awesome scientific results. In the course of his investigation he constructed a lens of great diameter out of one piece of glass by cutting out the central parts in successive ridges like stair steps. Thus was born an apparatus of then-unequaled power—the polyzonal lens—a lens constructed by building it on several circular segments. This useful discovery, which created light-stabs of brilliance that could pierce far into the night, was later perfected and named after French physicist A. Fresnel, and resulted in the lighthouse as we know it today.

Fresnel lens photographed at Chesapeake Maritime Museum, St. Michaels, Maryland. A colleague remarked, "Every lighthouse that burns round the shores of the British empire is a shining witness to the usefulness of Brewster's life."

This breakthrough was followed by yet other honors. Brewster was admitted to the Royal Society of London, and was later awarded the Rumford gold and silver medal for his theory on the polarization of light. Ambient light, which comprises most of the light we encounter every day, is a collection of light waves vibrating in all directions. When light is reflected or it passes through certain materials, the waves tend to vibrate in a single direction. Light that vibrates in this more orderly fashion is polarized. Brewster discovered a simple way to calculate the angle at which light must strike a substance for maximum polarization. Brewster's Angle is useful in all kinds of practical applications, from adjusting radio signals to building microscopes capable of examining objects on a molecular scale. It is central to the development of fiber optics, lasers, and to the study of meteorology, cosmology, and material science. Success followed success, and in 1816, the Institute of France adjudged him 3,000 francs—half the prizes given that year—for the two most important scientific discoveries made in the two previous years.

Then, as an added jewel to his already glittering optics crown, Brewster invented the kaleidoscope! It was 1816, and Brewster, at 35, was already an established philosopher, writer, scientist, and inventor. His kaleidoscope created unprecedented clamor. Dr. Peter M. Roget (whose illustrious *Thesaurus*, established in 1834, continues to be the most valued writer's tool next to the dictionary) paid tribute to his friend Sir David's invention in *Blackwood's Magazine* in 1818: "In the memory of man, no invention, and no work, whether addressed to the imagination or to the understanding, ever produced such an effect."

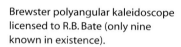

A universal mania for the instrument seized all classes, from the lowest to the highest, from the most ignorant to the most learned, and every person not only felt, but expressed the feeling that a new pleasure had been added to their existence.

While Brewster was granted a patent for his kaleidoscope (see page 132 for full patent), as well as acknowledgment and acclaim for his invention, he did not realize any remuneration. Others did, however. There was some fault with the patent registration, and before Brewster could claim any financial rewards, kaleidoscopes were quickly manufactured by aggressive entrepreneurs who sold hundreds of thousands with great financial success for themselves. As was the case for so many other great men, this was to be the pattern of Brewster's life: great intellectual achievement without worldly compensation.

Brewster polyangular kaleidoscope licensed to R.B. Bate (only nine known in existence).

Brewster telescopic kaleidoscope with extra cells, all surfaces silver plate. Licensed to I. Ruthven. Photo by Bill Carroll

In 1823, the Institute of France elected Brewster a corresponding member. The Royal Academies of Russia, Prussia, Sweden, and Denmark each conferred on him the highest distinctions accorded a foreigner. These high honors opened lines of communication for him with the great minds of Europe.

In midlife, in 1832, he was knighted by William IV, instantaneously acquiring a social status known only by those few touched by the king. However, Brewster simply continued to pursue his investigations and experiments. In short, he remained the poorly paid teacher whom James Hogg described in this manner: "He has indeed some minor specialities about him. For example, he holds that soda water is wholesomer drink than bottled beer, objects to a body's putting a nipper of spirits in their tea, and maintains that you ought to shave every morning, and wash your feet every night,—but who would wish to be severe on the eccentricities of genius?"[1]

Stobo Castle in Peeblesshire, Scotland, where Brewster signed his kaleidoscope patent August 27, 1817. It now operates as a fitness health resort.

[1]Letter from James Hogg to James Frazer, *Frazer's Magazine* for Town and Country, v. 6 Aug.-Dec. 1832.

One of Brewster's most illustrious moments came in 1849. He was nominated as one of a panel of eight foreign associates to the National Institute of France. So great were Brewster's achievements in comparison to all others that, after examination, the institute struck the names of all other candidates and Sir David Brewster stood in splendid isolation as the sole remaining candidate. His discoveries of the physical laws of metallic reflection and light absorption, the optical properties of crystals, and the law of the angle of polarization, along with his improvement of the stereoscope and lighthouse apparatus, surpassed most scientific achievements of that era.

Brewster's contributions to philosophy and science earned him honors and accolades from his peers, but it was by his pen that he earned his living. Among his most noteworthy books are two major treatises on the kaleidoscope (one written in 1816, and a revised edition in 1858); two separate biographies on the life of Sir Isaac Newton; *A Treatise on New Philosophical Instruments*; *Martyrs of Science: or the Laws of Galileo, Tycho, Brahe, and Kepler*; *Letters on Natural Magic Addressed to Sir Walter Scott*; *A Treatise on Optics*; and *More Worlds Than One*.

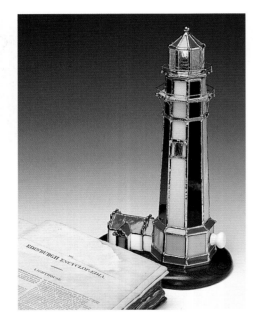

Original Edinburgh Encyclopedia Vol. "L" (1830). Kaleidoscope lighthouse, "Brewster's Cove", by Timothy Krause (1998). Photo by John Woodin

The bicentenary of Brewster's birth provided a suitable occasion to re-examine the history of this great man. A symposium was held at the Royal Scottish Museum in Edinburgh on November 21, 1981. Each segment of his diverse career was covered by an expert authority, and it was the general consensus that in a time and place renowned for artistic, intellectual, scientific, and technical vitality, Brewster's accomplishments were unsurpassed. Quoting from writer and Brewster colleague R. S. Westfall, "He deserves to be remembered as one of humanity's prouder exhibits. What an inexhaustible reservoir of vitality."[2]

There is no doubt that Brewster would be surprised and perhaps disillusioned to find that his most enduring legacy is the kaleidoscope. His achievements and contributions to the world of science, and to the social and cultural history of the era, actually covered a much broader spectrum, as did

[2]Proceedings of the complete symposium were published in "Martyr of Science, Sir David Brewster 1781-1868," Royal Scottish Museum, Edinburgh 1984.

his numerous inventions, including the lenticular stereoscope, binocular camera, polyzonal lens, polarimeter, and lighthouse illuminator.

AMERICAN INPUT: CHARLES G. BUSH (1825-1900)

ery little kaleidoscope activity was generated in America until 1873. The facts that one kaleidoscope was known to be made as early as 1818, or that one was exhibited in 1833 at the Franklin Institute in Philadelphia, rank low in the annals of kaleidoscope history compared to the memorable date of November 11, 1873. That exact date was stamped, along with "Patent Pending," on the brass endpiece of each parlor kaleidoscope by Charles G. Bush of Providence, Rhode Island.

Bush and Brewster kaleidoscopes.
Photo by John Woodin

Charles Bush

U.S. patent records list a number of new kaleidoscopes in those early years, but very few were actually produced. Many more patents were granted for various improvements to the kaleidoscope, but again only those pertaining to the Bush scopes were of lasting significance.

Several patents were granted to Bush in 1873 and 1874 for improvements. These included one for hermetically sealed liquid-filled ampules to be used in the object case, and a second for a means to add and subtract pieces from the object case without having to disassemble it. In addition, he developed a light source so both transparent and opaque objects could be viewed, as well as a color wheel that changed the background for the images; and still another was for a four-legged wooden stand that could be disassembled for easy handling.

To find a Bush scope in good condition is quite rare, but if one does surface, it is more likely to be the single pedestal than the four-pronged model. And while it is rare indeed to find one with the wire attachment to hold a color card, the hole through which the wire passed is one sure way to recognize an original Bush. One unusual piece found occasionally in the object case of an original Bush scope is a clear glass disc embossed with a swan.

But it is the liquid-filled ampules that are by far the most distinctive feature of the Bush scope. Inside the liquids are air bubbles that continue to move even after the object case is at rest.

While Bush has been given credit for the first liquid-filled ampules, there is mention in Brewster's original 1819 *Treatise* that "differently colored fluids enclosed and moving in small vessels of glass will make the finest transparent objects for the kaleidoscope."

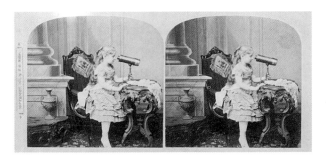

Contents of Bush cell, including liquid-filled ampules. Photo courtesy of Lew Sprague

Stereo views of young girl looking in Bush scope. Photo courtesy of Bill Carroll

That explains why a few such objects can be seen in some early European scopes.

Very little was written about Charles Bush, and it is only from his obituary that a few facts can be gleaned. Bush was an immigrant who came to the United States in 1847 from Colberg, Prussia, where he was born in 1825. Like Brewster, Bush did not expend energy in a single direction. Unlike Brewster, however, he was untrained in any of the physical sciences. Among the interests he pursued were the studies of microscopes, telescopes, astronomy, and photography. Bush used these by making and developing the increasingly popular stereoscope views.

Bush began manufacturing kaleidoscopes in the early 1870s. The quality and uniqueness of his parlor scopes were recognized and appreciated even then. He continued to make these instruments by the thousands until his death at the age of 75.

Bush kaleidoscope (c.1873).

Old toy scopes from the collection of David Meelheim

Variations of the Artascope, courtesy of David Meelheim

TOY INTERIM

During the years between its invention in the early 1800s and the renaissance in the late 1900s, the kaleidoscope has gone through many transformations. It has served as a toy for children, a parlor entertainment for adults, and a design palette for artists, jewelers, architects, weavers, and any profession in which ornamental patterns are required.

The popularity of the kaleidoscope first peaked during the Victorian era, when no elegant home was complete without a parlor scope for family entertainment. Then as the electronic age of radio and TV advanced, kaleidoscope sales decreased and they were relegated to the shelves of five and dime stores. One company stands out as the main link that kept kaleidoscope interest alive—the Steven Manufacturing Company. This toy business, started in 1946 and still operating today, has made hundreds of different versions of the kaleidoscope and manufactured hundreds of thousands of the popular toys, thereby spawning more scope collectors, perhaps, than any other single source. Many collectors concentrate on finding and trading the old Steven scopes.

"I have been collecting Steven scopes for 10 years," Lew Sprague explains, "and I'm still thrilled when I find another unknown model or one I don't have. I guess it brings out the kid in me. But it's great when a friend recalls a Steven scope from his childhood while looking at my collection."

Steven toys from the collection of Lew Sprague. Photo courtesy of Lew Sprague

KALEIDOSCOPE RENAISSANCE

The kaleidoscope echoes a lingering sense of what used to be • splendor and enchantment pure of vistas unimagined opens it as come to things of aura an with interlaced

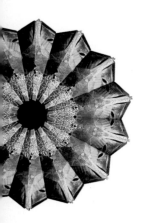

he kaleidoscope has recaptured the heart and imagination of America. Its unprecedented revival was born out of a nostalgic need for quiet beauty and a deep respect for the highest degree of craftsmanship. Through its various phases of manufacture the kaleidoscope has retained an element of magic, the promise of surprise, and has always inspired a sense of wonder. The instrument itself has developed and advanced by leaps and bounds: from a Victorian version of a video game to sculptural space-age spectaculars; from a toy to a new art form. While Brewster predicted his invention would be of great benefit to all the ornamental arts, there was no way he could foresee its becoming such a scintillating ornament of art itself.

Although scores of patents were granted between 1873 and 1973, scarcely any examples of kaleidoscopes made during this period remain in existence. There are several notable contrasts between the first kaleidoscopes

Opposite: Wiley Jobe's polyangular scope in four styles: "Bristol," chairside; "Eastlake," floor model; "Victoria," table model; and "Polystar," handheld. Photo by John Woodin

and today's state-of-the-art instruments: (1) The inventor was first and foremost a scientist, whereas the majority of contemporary designers are first and foremost artists. (2) While Brewster discovered and developed the kaleidoscope as an incidental part of his work as a research scientist, many of today's makers create scopes from a compelling urge to express themselves. (3) Finally, Brewster licensed his patent to others, and did not make the scopes himself. This differs greatly with the serious scope makers of today who take great pride in making every single element of the scope by hand —some even tooling the nuts and bolts, while a few go so far as to fabricate their own tools.

Van Dyke Series II by Bill O'Connor and the late Craig Musser stands alone as both an artistic achievement and a historic replica. It is a modern version of Bush's parlor scope with the added luster of first-surface mirrors and the artistry of a master glass blower.

The kaleidoscope renaissance had its earliest stirrings in the late 1970s. Among the first to reintroduce the kaleidoscope as art were Steven Auger, Carolyn Bennett, Peach Reynolds, Carol and Tom Paretti, Doug Johnson, Howard Chesshire, Charles Karadimos, Dorothea Marshall, Bill O'Connor, and the late Craig Musser and Judith Karelitz.

By far the most noteworthy kaleidoscope of the early revival was the Van Dyke Series II. The day Craig Musser took an antique Bush scope to Bill O'Connor for repair turned out to be a red letter day for the kaleidoscope world. O'Connor, a renowned glass blower and color impresario, was immediately inspired to make larger, more colorful, and ornate liquid-filled ampules, and to replace the cardboard barrel with an appropriate brass housing.

Their objective was not to reproduce a Bush scope exactly, but to design a more magnificent instrument, with greatly improved blown-glass objects. Thus began an extended period of serious research and development. By studying Brewster's patent and experimenting with drawing, pulling, and twisting shards of glass, Bill O'Connor perfected these small visionary vessels. He developed his own methods of hermetically sealing and encasing tiny crystals within the ampules. Not content to use existing colors of glass, Bill used mineral compounds in his glass-blowing furnaces to create his own

Image through Van Dyke Series II
by Craig Musser & Bill O'Connor.
Photo by Barbi Richardson

brilliant shades of cobalt blue, emerald green, ruby red, golden yellow, and fiery opalescent. He then designed a handsome pedestal scope worthy of his creative glass objects.

Series I was a small edition of five, most of which were given to family members; then came Series II, an edition of 50. The chief difference between the kaleidoscopes of the two series was the addition of a handsome presentation stand with a brass lamp. The $3,800 price tag did not deter appreciative collectors, even though the most expensive alternative at that time was only $285. O'Connor's use of surface reflection mirrors as early as 1979, and his fluoride-coated magnifying lens, along with other subtle quality controls, provided the sharp and vibrant optics needed for a truly fine scope. Number one from this series went to royalty for use on a yacht. Although the edition was sold out years ago, if and when one becomes available, the going price is likely to be closer to $10,000.

Wooden parlour scope with extra cells by Carol & Tom Paretti

The other early kaleidoscope renaissance artists provided significant and varied contributions: Steven Auger orchestrated color harmonics in his object cells. Judith Karelitz was the first to work with polarized light material and filters. Carolyn Bennett used her original artwork for the exterior of her scopes and introduced the first wearable scope. Doug Johnson was the first to use clear and beveled glass for the bodies of his scopes. Among other major firsts to his credit were the binocular scope and the use of marbles for the viewing objects. Howard Chesshire included three double convex lenses, a prism, and discrete space in his 16" "Mandala" teleidoscopes.

Carol and Tom Paretti were among the first to fashion scopes from finely hewn, smoothly rubbed, and painstakingly polished exotic hardwoods. Peach Reynolds invented the Camerascope, and a brass battery-operated, sound-activated scope. Dorothea Marshall was the first to use Austrian crystals for the viewing objects, and the first to use oil-filled cells. Charles Karadimos

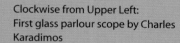

Clockwise from Upper Left:
First glass parlour scope by Charles Karadimos

Kaleidoscopes by Doug & Dottie Johnson of Windseye

Acrylic scopes by Carolyn Bennett. Photo by Peter Groesbeck

Champlevé scopes by Stephen Auger

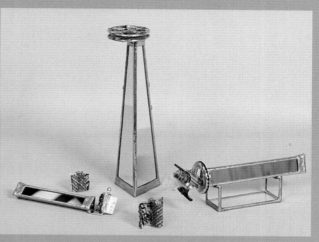

Strathmore Hall Art Center, North Bethesda, Maryland, site of the world's first kaleidoscope exhibition. Photo by John Woodin of painting by John P. Eberhard

was one of the first to experiment with every degree on the compass to demonstrate the varieties of symmetry in kaleidoscope imagery. He also devoted time to mastering the art of perfect optics.

While most kaleidoscope makers work alone or with one partner, usually in a home studio, one pioneering couple decided to go into production in a big way. Erik and Kate Van Cort have been in the business of making optical instruments since 1979 and kaleidoscopes since 1983. Their greatest strength is in the mechanical arts. They design and deliver quality products from their spacious New England workshop where they may employ up to a hundred people at any given time. Among their most popular kaleidoscopes are an authentic reproduction of the Charles G. Bush kaleidoscope and the phenomenally successful "Dragonfly."

The renaissance gained momentum in the 1980s with an article in the November, 1982 *Smithsonian Magazine*, followed by publication in 1985 of the first book on the subject, *Through the Kaleidoscope* by Cozy Baker, and the world's first exhibition of kaleidoscopes at Strathmore Hall Arts Center in Bethesda, Maryland. Then, in 1986, Cozy Baker founded the Brewster Society, an international organization for kaleidoscope enthusiasts.

Game table with kaleidoscopes in Brewster Society's house/museum. Photo by John Woodin

This unique organization has probably been the most remarkable offshoot of the kaleidoscope renaissance. The Brewster Society is a living, breathing kaleidoscope of mutually motivated seekers of beauty. They find beauty not only in the kaleidoscopes, but in the people who make, sell, and collect them. There are no officers other than the founding president—no boards, no rules and regulations, nor by-laws. Its purpose is to enjoy kaleidoscopes and the company of fellow scope-lovers. The Society publishes a quarterly newsletter, holds an annual convention, and maintains a museum for the exclusive use of its members. Kaleidoscopes generate a community of interest that forges a strong bond. It is this connecting bond between members that is the very heart of the Brewster Society.

During the 1990s, the kaleidoscope revival accelerated to full speed as leading artists developed new techniques and experimented with complicated mirror arrangements. Many new designers joined the ranks, adding their own individual innovations. Fine craft and gift shops and a few art galleries added scopes to their inventories. Then a couple of "how-to" books lured would-be kaleidoscopists to jump on the scope-wagon!

And now, as an established new art form, the kaleidoscope is poised to fulfill its important role in the cultural transformation predicted for the third millennium—to assist in a renewed awareness of beauty and the discovery of new insights.

Tiffany stained glass windows at Knollwood Mausoleum in Cleveland, Ohio. Photographed by Joe Polevoi, the photo at left taken through a Reynolds Camerascope

What is the kaleidoscope's compelling fascination for collectors? There is no particular type of person or profession that seems more attracted to them than another—political or religious persuasion certainly isn't a factor, nor is background, nationality, or age, and as many men as women find collecting them irresistible.

Author Bill Novak offers the following explanation: "As for me, I prefer to collect them for the sheer fun of it. I like art that moves, and that I can actually touch. If pressed, I'll admit to enjoying the paradox that kaleidoscopes exemplify—while they allow you more control than other forms of art, to fully appreciate them you have to surrender. You can change the image as often as you like, but you never know what's coming next. The lesson here, I think, is that nothing in life is immune to change, and that what counts is how we react to it. With enough patience, the fragments in our personal object chambers can be coaxed into any number of new arrangements."

Contemporary scopes from the collection of Cynthia Donahue

Cynthia Donahue has been collecting scopes for about twelve years. She says, "They bring back magical mystical moments from my childhood—dreams of lost paradises, and ecstasies."

Ann Franklin never leaves home without one! In fact, she travels to elder hostels around the world with a suitcase-full of scopes. When she isn't teaching a group how to make them, she just enjoys sharing them with fellow elders.

Pat Seaman has been collecting kaleidoscopes for thirty years. The Ernst Trova "Falling Man Kaleidoscope" was her first purchase, and she recalls taking it with her on a train trip through East Germany during the late 1960s and sharing it with an elderly couple. "We spoke not a word of the other's language, but there were smiles and gestures that were our common language, and we recognized our human spirit link."

Renaissance kaleidoscopes at the home of collector Linda Joy. Photo by John Woodin

Corner shelving in the "kaleidocave" at the home of Vince and Rhea Cianfichi

Linda Joy discovered the allure of kaleidoscopes while selling them at The Red Balloon in Washington, D.C., twenty years ago. Since then she has learned to appreciate them even more, and finds them to be emotionally fulfilling "through the low luster of sadness to the heights of joyous love."

Collector Vince Cianfichi is convinced that "a true kaleidoscope connoisseur is the only one who can understand and appreciate the feelings, enjoyment and motivations of his fellow collector." Vince and his wife, Rhea, admit they love collecting scopes for the pure enjoyment of collecting as well as for the fascination of the kaleidoscopes themselves. They relish the hunt —and love seeking the rare and unusual during their travels. "With each kaleidoscope we collect, a new story is made," Vince explains, "telling more about ourselves and our travels." It was only natural that in building a new home, they designed a special space (which they refer to as their "kaleido-cave") to showcase their collection.

A close-up of "Through the Roof" in the dining room ceiling at Bruce Haney's home. Photo by Jim Scholz

Bruce Haney, a stock broker and financial advisor in Omaha, Nebraska, commissioned a kaleidoscope artist to install a scope in the ceiling of his dining room. To those who ask if he thinks they are a good investment, Bruce answers, "Instead of thinking about the kaleidoscope's future appreciation, I just appreciate its daily dividends of beauty and relaxation."

While designing her new home in California, art conservator Judith Paul included many special features to accommodate her growing kaleidoscope collection. "I suspect one reason I am so attracted to kaleidoscopes," she confides, "is because they are both a right- and left-brain activity. They are not alive without the art and they are no good without perfect optics. It is the combination of both disciplines that makes them (for me) endlessly fascinating."

Music professor Solie Fott says the scope's appeal to him is two-fold. Equally important to the beauty of the interior image is the incomparable craftsmanship and ingenuity of the exterior. His collection kept growing until he found it necessary to build a special room for space and to provide proper lighting.

Scopes from collector Solie Fott's kaleidoscope room

Quilter Paula Nadelstern sheds light on a completely different reason for collecting kaleidoscopes. "There are two kinds of surprises: the meticulously planned kind and the happy coincidence. Making kaleidoscope quilts allows me to synthesize elements of both, to merge control and spontaneity to spark something unexpected. There is an air of abracadabra as the last seam is stitched because the whole is truly greater than the sum of its parts. And in the end, I am both the one who makes the magic and the one who is surprised."

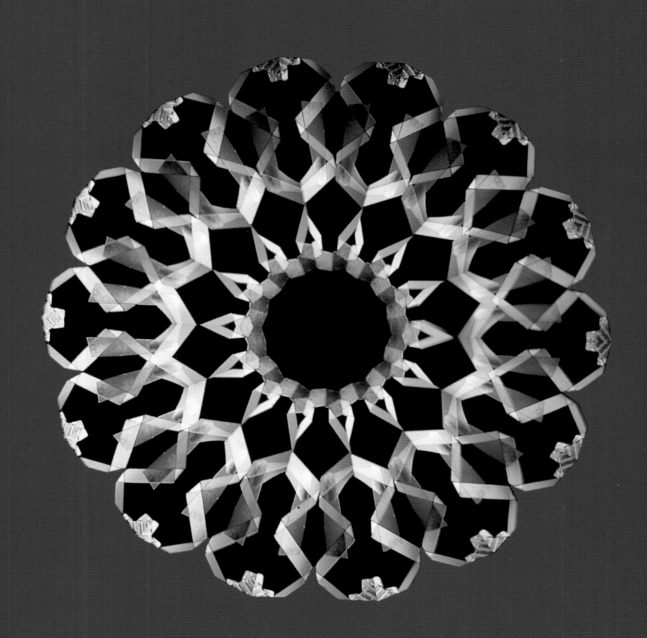

MEDITATIVE AND THERAPEUTIC VALUE

Kaleidoscopes are reminders that beauty shines forth from within . . . . . they provide music and poetry for the eyes, and a rich feast for the soul

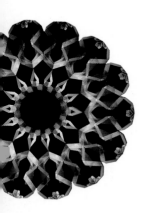

The kaleidoscope renaissance is more than a revival of interest in a captivating collectible. Beyond a marriage of science and art, it is a marriage of sense and soul. The kaleidoscope's imagery is a form of art that can influence the way you think, the way you feel, and the way you react. By focusing on the images, you can help cultivate your entire being: spirit, mind, and body. Senses are immersed and energy is renewed, leading to a more conscious, centered, and creative life.

The promise of ever-evolving beauty and order is the kaleidoscope's indelible message of hope. Moments of life begin to take on new meaning when we find a few minutes each day to sit quietly and gaze into a kaleidoscope with a "listening" eye. Daily meditation reunites the soul and the spirit. It reveals complete balance, harmony, and oneness with the Divine Being, the source of all light.

To fully perceive and appreciate the import of the kaleidoscope's hidden splendors, one must withdraw to the innermost temple of color. Calm all busy, active thoughts. Open the windows of your mind and welcome breezes

Opposite: Magnolia tree in Cleveland, normal view and through a C. Bennett scopelens™, photographed by Joe Polevoi

The kaleidoscope is a
brilliant palette of
mandalas

a spectrum of positive
energies abrim with hope

With no beginnings and
no endings

each dissolving image
regenerates itself

into its own creation

communicating new
beauty

from the breakup and
rearrangement

of what came before

Random fragments
interlace and meld

ever-changing—
but constant

unpredictable—
yet reliably beautiful

forever resulting in
perfect symmetry

as each piece—
no matter how small

fulfills its essential part
of the whole

of inspiration. Breathe each color, concentrating on the ones that soothe the soul and touch the heart. Contemplate the illumination within, and embrace each image.

In 1949, S.G.J. Ousley wrote a beautiful little volume on developing color consciousness, *Colour Meditations, with Guide to Colour-Healing* (L.N. Fowler & Co. Ltd., London). Each of the 31 meditations is comprised of two parts. The following meditation combines the Visualization of number 20 and the Realization of number 15:

"Kaleidoscopia," color pencil drawing by Betty Tribe

Visualize a radiant sunset of flame-colours and purple, the whole Western sky shot with every shade of crimson and gold and amethyst. Picture the sun sinking slowly down behind the rim of the world. The vast radiation stretches far out, embracing everything and reaching toward the East where the sky is full of heavenly turquoise. Every little cloud is flushed with purest rose, the cosmic emblem of Divine Love.

Realization: Love and beauty are keynotes of the universe. The value of colours is that they possess a power of vibration of their own that differs according to the quality and radiation. Thus positive or magnetic colours have the effect of awakening in our souls feelings and powers akin to themselves. When feeling depressed or discouraged, anxious or depleted, you should visualize red (courage and strength), green (hope and faith), scarlet (victory), emerald (joy), bright blue (happiness), yellow (guidance and wisdom), amethyst (spiritual awareness). You will find that your inner soul, the real source of your thoughts and health, responds to the power and vibration of the rays. Without the uplifting and inspiring influence of colour our minds would be perpetually in a state of darkness and turmoil.

MANDALA AND METAPHOR

There are those who see the small miracles unfolding within a kaleidoscope as reflections of a higher infinite beauty. They sense a divine order in the harmonious perfection. The imagery lives, equating itself to the age-old mandala.

A mandala is a circular symbol of wholeness. It is a circle expanding from its individual center as it interrelates with other circles, each radiating from its center, all being one with a creative universal source. Examples of mandalas can be observed all around us, from the iris of our own eyes to the heavenly bodies, and from the procession of the seasons to the cycle of life and death. Carl Jung referred to the mandala as "eternal mind's eternal re-creation" and the "mirror of our becoming whole."

Kaleidoscope artist David Kalish feels there is something deep within our nature that universally responds to this impeccable order of symmetry. "In symmetry there is a balance; in balance there is harmony; in harmony, equilibrium. As long as we are perfectly balanced, we cannot fall. As long as we do not fall, we continue to survive. Survival is the ultimate and perpetual striving of all living things, from the most primitive to the most sophisticated being. Somewhere therein lies the relationship between the universal appeal of kaleidoscope mandalas, the inspiration of beauty, the wonder of nature, and the awesome magnificence of Creation itself."

A few other scope artists answer the question, "What does the mandala mean to you?"

Stained glass at Scripps Library in San Diego, photographed by Joe Polevoi, normal view and through a Reynolds camerascope

Will Smith **It is like the beating of a heart. It is what gives a scope its life.**

Dean Krause **It is like a world unto itself, a universal element that talks to me in ways that words cannot. It is a symbol of something and is, simultaneously, the thing it represents.**

Janice Chesnik **It represents continuity, beauty, and serenity, but holding the possibility of something new and exciting with every change, just like life itself.**

Glenn Straub **Centering, along with consciousness expansion, enables the kaleidoscope viewer to expand beyond a close personal situation in order to reach a comprehensive view of the universal.**

Doug Johnson **Mandala images are calming, refreshing, and, being entirely nonverbal, are not reminders of other tasks, ideas, or associations. Hence, they allow everyone to find in a dynamic way the colors, patterns, moods, and images that are most pleasing to them, in a way producing beautiful works that are most expressive of their inner desires and wishes.**

Kaleidoscope artist Howard Chesshire and his bride Faye gave me permission to reveal how their lives are totally intertwined with the mandala in the meaningful words of their wedding vows:

I have loved you since I met you,
And now I know that I will love you forever
We are Northern Lights
My mirror, My Mandala, Our Art.

This is the threshold
Beyond is the calm of knowing forever,
Growing together—
Living and loving together forever

I will hold your head, heart, hands, and health
I will feel and massage your body.
I will excite your mind.
I will fulfill your expectations.

I will create rainbows in your shower.
I will create crystals in your snow.
I will create color in your sunshine.
I will embroider your lifelight with glow.

We have spun our certainty,
Found our faith and lost our fears.
We will become a circle,
A unity to float through all the years—
My life is ours—a mandala.

Computer-generated color chords, pigmented ink on canvas by Brian Evans

Of all the many facets of the kaleidoscope, perhaps the most significant is that of metaphor. On a personal level, each life is a kaleidoscope, full of unpredictable, but constant change. "Kaleidoscope of Tomorrow: Ours to Design" was the theme for the 1992 Conference of Sisters of Charity Health Care Systems. The following lines were printed in their liturgy: "When a kaleidoscope is held to the light, it is the light that brings the pattern together. It is the Lord of Light who allows different patterns to emerge through the kaleidoscope of each of our lives. It is through individual and communal reflection that we are able to see these patterns and designs more clearly."

Linda Montgomery says it in the following poem.

LIFE IS A KALEIDOSCOPE

Changing patterns, changing concepts, changing colors,
The kaleidoscope of my being is shifting.

New life is emerging.
Like a growing seed pushing up through the soil.
There is struggle, change, transformation.
I am called to let go of the past.
I am drawn into the newness of this moment,
To seek the beauty of each kaleidoscopic pattern,
To acknowledge the gift of each experience,
And to let it go.

Bits of colored glass are rearranging themselves
And I glimpse the perfection of symmetry.
I cannot preserve the pattern.
However carefully I put down the kaleidoscope,
The pattern changes.
What is it that makes me want time to stand still?
I fear that the gold I hold in my hand will turn to sand,
That the road I am following will find its end.

"Flowers Real and Imagined"
by Irene Holler

I am reminded of God's loving presence.
If I live in the consciousness of Love,
Each moment can be more beautiful than the last.
Life then becomes a collection of precious gems,
Not bits and pieces of colored glass.
I feel the deep blue peace of sapphire,
The passion of rubies,
The healing green of emeralds.

Sometimes I search for treasure, and yet,
If I am calm and poised,
The gift in each moment is revealed.
I am called to acknowledge these gifts.
Each lesson, each experience, allows me to become
Something greater.

When I'm most lost and confused,
It's helpful to remember—
My life is a kaleidoscope
Of changing thoughts and patterns,
Evolving into a multi-faceted perspective.
Then the colored glass
Becomes precious gems of joy, and truth,
Harmony and balance,
Rearranging themselves
So I can stretch and expand and reach for the Light.

And for the bigger picture, the world is a kaleidoscope. Dr. Ruth R. Middleman, a professor of social work at the University of Louisville, uses this very metaphor in a book she co-authored with fellow-professor Gary B. Rhodes, *Competent Supervision: Making Imaginative Judgments.*

Our world is a kaleidoscope... It and we move and flow continuously, with certain unexpected, potentially diverse patterns and configurations. But the pattern may pop into a totally new arrangement as we notice and manipulate it and ourselves....This is a world where fluctuations are central and change moves from disorder to higher levels of order, recurrent random fluctuations lead to order through selective choice, to a new order out of chaos. This world involves instabilities and fluctuations; understanding it requires looking at the whole cycle, the totality...the patterns that the kaleidoscope accentuates, remind us to keep seeking the shifting meanings, the patterns which recur, albeit in new configurations....

So we return to our world view captured as a tumbling kaleidoscope whose pieces and elements continuously move and shift so long as there is life force, turbulence, and restlessness. We believe we have used a congenial metaphor to suggest the 'big picture', one that has inherent changeableness, beauty, and whimsy as its characteristics.[1]

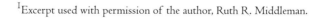

"Upper Grand Canyon Gouache"
by Irene Holler

Kaleidoscope artist Dean Kent also sees the multifaceted mural of the world as a kaleidoscope:

The kaleidoscopes we are making today are motivated by an inner necessity to create and reflect the unfolding growth in our own lives. Too often people concentrate on the differences and problems that exist between us rather than acknowledging the universality of human experience. We believe the kaleidoscope can best be understood as a metaphor for a new world perspective. It is as if you took the multiplicity of people, places, and things in the world and placed them in an object case. Where there was division, difference, and chaos, there emerges integration, similarity, and resolution.

The metaphor offers the hope of a connecting, purposeful spirit that envelops the earth, relating all organisms in an endless chain of life. The simple pleasure of viewing a kaleidoscope reminds us of the interdependence of life on earth. The earth as seen from space is a living mandala, an organic whole, and as an image, forms a foundation for a widening of the human perceptual horizon and a broadening of thought and understanding.

R. Scott Cole, kaleidoscope artist, teacher, and psychological counselor, adds his idea of kaleidoscope as metaphor: "A kaleidoscope can provide a creative beauty that continues to change; one cannot 'replay' a pattern. Thus a kaleidoscope serves not as an escape from conflict but as a tool for generating

[1]Excerpt used with permission of the author, Ruth R. Middleman.

greater acceptance and harmony. Perhaps this serves as a metaphor of life—beauty and change, but you can't turn back."

Therapist Nitya Prema succinctly sums up her view of this metaphor: "We are each a part of the divine kaleidoscope of the universe. Like the labyrinth, kaleidoscopes evoke an understanding of our relationship with the whole. Once the microscope was a symbol for the expansion of human consciousness. Then the telescope became symbolic of our visionary minds. Now in the midst of our changing and multidimensional world we have the kaleidoscope as metaphor. I envision it opening our hearts and minds to seeing the beauty in the infinite pattern that connects us all."

THERAPY

Interior of "Spikey Planet" by Marc Tickle

Mental rest is as important to our overall health as physical relaxation, and kaleidoscopes are an excellent source of mental rest. By its very stillness and quiet, the experience of kaleidoscope viewing helps reduce stress and promotes tranquil reflection. It is virtually impossible to harbor negative thoughts or feelings while looking into a kaleidoscope, which automatically saves wear and tear on one's emotions and body tension.

There are physicians, dentists, and psychiatrists who keep scopes in their waiting rooms to help relieve a patient's anxiety. (A few lawyers have even been known to keep them on hand for relieving stress among contentious clients.) Scopes are also used by therapists to divert hyperactivity in troubled children, and as a vehicle for them to participate in the creative process.

The very act of making kaleidoscopes proves therapeutic for at least one artist. It was while working as a pediatric oncology nurse that Sherry Moser learned to look at the world in a different way. A hospital chaplain, teaching the staff how to reduce stress, likened each person to a bucket filled with water from which we dip to give of ourselves. He explained that we dip and dip until, if we are not careful, our bucket becomes empty. "He was trying to teach us to take care of ourselves," Sherry observed, "so that our buckets would not become empty. Making kaleidoscopes became my way of refilling my bucket. Creating something beautiful is a good way to relieve tension, and of course the scopes themselves bring tranquility and peace needed to balance a stressful life."

Lisa and Cru Chase of upstate New York have initiated Project (K)aleidoscope, through which they use the kaleidoscope as a learning tool to improve students' self-esteem, build a sense of community, link curriculum areas, and produce academic results.

Lisa affirms the purpose of Project K is to "awaken good feelings about learning, to validate students' belief that learning can be exciting, and the more exciting a project or work is, the better it is performed." Project K also helps students learn to trust and use their imaginations, and to work together. "They learn that amazing things can happen and that opportunities are out there just waiting to be taken," Lisa explains. "In order for underachieving students to meet standards of excellence, they need to believe that they, with their unique gifts, talents and intelligence, can make a difference. This is the wonder of Project K."

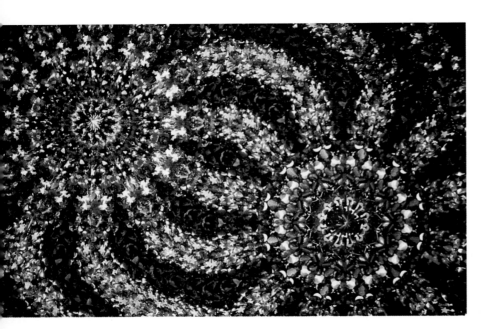

"Yin Yang" by David Sugich

The response of one student proves the worth of such a project: "Never before has anyone taken the time to hear what I had to say, or how I felt about things. This project was one of the first times in my life I didn't feel like an outcast. Not once did I feel inferior to anyone. I learned a lot about a lot of things: math, English, science, history, computers, and how to work with people. Most of all, thank you for letting me use my imagination. I never created anything before, and never thought I could. But I learned that when you work together in a group, amazing things can happen!" (written by "A.C.")

As a registered art therapist and art educator with twenty-five years of experience, Dr. Beverly Scheiffer highly recommends the use of kaleidoscope projects in working with a variety of special populations. "Kaleidoscope patterns offer unparalleled opportunities for the study of art elements such as the principles of form and color, harmony, and problem solving through constant emergence of order from chaos, all of which allow students to participate in the creative process which is restorative, relaxing, stress-reducing, spirit-enhancing and gratifying."

Ned Herrmann, director of the Whole Brain Corp., finds kaleidoscopes a wonderful tool in determining "right" or "left" brain dominance. He points out that, "The turning of a kaleidoscope symbolizes the rearranging of stored information to constantly create new patterns, new approaches to problem solving."

The kaleidoscope's ability to soothe and stimulate at the same time makes it a perfect tool for balance. Dr. Clifford Kuhn, a psychiatrist in the Department of Psychiatry and Behavioral Sciences at the University of Kentucky, writes:

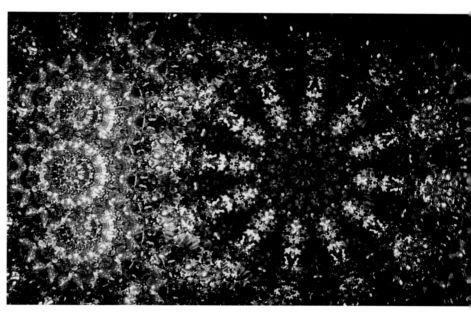

"Insight" (Cathedral) by David Sugich

The essence of health is wholeness, an integration of body, mind, and spirit in equilibrium. Medical research has revealed that many of our current illnesses are the result of the effect of stress. Stress is destructive to our body, disorganizing to our mind, and disabling to our spirit. It has been demonstrated that a regular habit of quietly drawing aside from one's usual responsibilities for reflection and relaxation significantly repairs or prevents the potentially destructive effects of daily stress.

Kaleidoscope viewing is one such activity of repair. It is restorative to the body in that it requires physical stillness and stimulates pleasant visual sensations. At the same time it has a beneficial effect on the mind by presenting an endless variety of form and color combinations that stir the imagination and stimulate the intellect. Kaleidoscopes are, likewise, good medicine to the spirit as they reflect the constant emergence of order out of disorder and provide a sense of participation in the creative process. In this way, regular viewing of kaleidoscopes can be a significant contributor to a person's overall health.

Kaleidoscopes are being used in an increasing number of cancer clinics and hospices. One hospice nurse states, "It helps both the patient and the

Above: "Kushan Water Urns" by Irene Holler

Upper Right: "Sylvan Wonderland" painting by Barbara Mitchell. Photo by Bob Gregson, Wonderland Studio

care giver, even if it is just for a short while, to transcend pain by experiencing beauty." Another nurse at a cancer clinic points out, "There is something incredibly wonderful about how kaleidoscopes help revive a sense of wonder in terminally ill patients."

Nitya Prema turned her energies from designing kaleidoscopes to using them as "medicine for the soul" in her work with older people. "A big part of my job as social worker and therapist is to help patients rekindle and rediscover their interests and sense of purpose," she explains. "In addition to being an antidote for tension and stress, kaleidoscopes have a way of reaching the most withdrawn and even mentally disorganized patients. Looking through scopes helps bring out their deeper hidden stories, and enables them to reminisce, sometimes coming to grips with unfinished experiences."

The folklorist Sabine Baring-Gould found these verses in a Cambridge University undergraduates' magazine published in the nineteenth century, and they were reprinted in *Competent Supervision: Making Imaginative Judgments*, by Ruth H. Middleman and Gary B. Rhodes:

I was just five years old, that December,
And a fine little promising boy.
So my grandmother said, I remember.
And gave me a strange-looking toy:
In its shape it was lengthy and rounded,
It was papered with yellow and blue.
One end with a glass top was bounded.
At the other, a hole to look through.

'Dear Granny, what's this?' I came crying,
'A box for my pencils? But see,
I can't open it hard though I'm trying,
O what is it? What can it be?'
'Why, my dear, if you only look through it,
And stand with your face to the light;
Turn it gently (that's just how to do it!),
And you'll see a remarkable sight.'
'O how beautiful!' cried I, delighted,
As I saw each fantastic device,
The bright fragments now closely united,
All falling apart in a trice.

"Florentine I" by Irene Holler

Times have passed, and new years will now find me,
Each birthday, no longer a boy.
Yet me thinks that their turns may remind me
of the turns of my grandmother's toy.
For in all this world, with its beauties,
Its pictures so bright and so fair,
You may vary the pleasures and duties
But still, the same pieces are there.

From the time that the earth was first founded,
There has never been anything new,
The same thoughts, the same things, have redounded
Till the colours have pall'd on the view.
But though all that is old is returning,
There is yet in this sameness a change;
And new truths are the wise ever learning,
For the patterns must always be strange.
Shall we say that our days are all weary?
All labour, and sorrow, and care,
That its pleasures and joys are but dreary,
Mere phantoms that vanish in air?
Ah, no! There are some darker pieces,
And others transparent and bright;
But this, surely, the beauty increases,
Only stand with your face to the light.
And the treasures for which we are yearning,
Those joys, now succeeded by pain
Are but spangles, just hid in the turning;
They will come to the surface again.

DIVERSITY OF EXTERIOR DESIGNS

Each kaleidoscope sings its own song and empowers moments of solitude · happiness your own feel self your lets It glory. and calm With

ith more colors than a rainbow and patterns as numerous as the stars, kaleidoscopes are being fashioned into every conceivable shape and form, from simplistic to stupendous. There are scopes one can wear, smell, listen to, and feel. There are simple cardboard tubes with metallic mirrors containing plastic bits and pieces, and there are tubes made of sterling silver and 14 kt. gold set with rubies and emeralds. It is astounding that one basic concept involving a simple set of mirrors, with an eyepiece at one end and an object cell at the other, can produce such a limitless variety of creative ingenuity.

There are five major types of kaleidoscopes: teleidoscope, cell scope, wheel scope, marble or sphere, and projection. The endpiece (cell, wheel, marble, etc.) determines the type.

Opposite Top: Glass scopes by Allen Crandell, Debra Davis, Gordon & Analeise Redmond, Sue Ross, Carmen & Stephen Colley, Greg Hanks. Photo by John Woodin

Opposite Bottom: Triangular metal scope by Ken & Dore Wilhoite; rectangular wooden scope by Nash Gallo; circular wood and glass scope by Andrew Leary. Photo by John Woodin

1. TELEIDOSCOPE There is no endpiece containing color, only a clear lens that turns everything it is pointed toward into a kaleidoscopic image.

Teleidoscope

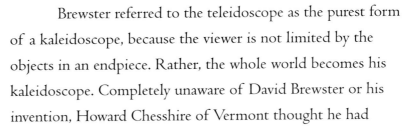

Brewster referred to the teleidoscope as the purest form of a kaleidoscope, because the viewer is not limited by the objects in an endpiece. Rather, the whole world becomes his kaleidoscope. Completely unaware of David Brewster or his invention, Howard Chesshire of Vermont thought he had invented the teleidoscope in 1973 after he had experimented with mirrors and lenses for four years. On learning of its invention 150 years earlier, Chesshire was still convinced that "the ultimate value of the teleidoscope is the potential each viewer has to see the artistic value in his own environment."

Most teleidoscopes contain a simple equilateral three-mirror arrangement. However, every mirror system used in a standard kaleidoscope can also be used in a teleidoscope. Corki Weeks has probably experimented with more different mirror systems in a teleidoscope than anyone else, even placing two different arrangements in the same instrument; she also made one teleidoscope into a necklace. Jack Lazarowski and Tim Grannis of Prism Design created the ultimate limited-edition teleidoscope. "The Gallery" is a sculptural assemblage of five separate scopes, each with a different optical image, and removable from a lighted base.

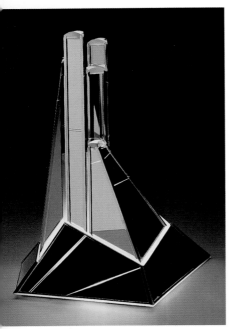

"The Gallery" by Prism Designs

2. CELL SCOPE The endpiece is an enclosed case containing colored objects (also called object case or chamber). Cells can be:
dry-filled with tumbling pieces (front or side-lit)
liquid-filled with floating pieces (front or side-lit)
polarized light material and filters
empty to allow personal choice of items
tubes—elongated clear case with floating items in liquid

Cell scope

There are more cell scopes than any other type. The many moving pieces provide the most varied and nonrepetitive imagery. There is also more variety in the cell itself: clear, frosted, or etched; recessed, flush, or protruding; black backdrop, side-lit; and liquid-filled. Increasingly popular are the cells that can be opened to include favorite objects. Bob McWilliam makes all of his cells with this added feature. One was used for a marriage proposal, with the inclusion of an engagement ring and the words, "Will you marry me?"

The space tube (or wand) is probably the most duplicated scope in the world. WildeWood Creative Products (in collaboration with Cozy Baker) was the first to produce this type of scope as the "Illusion" in 1990, and the "Grand Illusion" in 1998. Since then almost everyone who has ever tried making a scope of any kind has used some sort of liquid-filled tube with sparkling bits and pieces as the object. No matter which mirror system is used, the image resembles flashing fireworks. David Sugich developed a technique that transforms the wand scope into a three-dimensional wonderland of flowers, butterflies, or angels.

3. WHEEL SCOPE One, two, or more wheels comprise the endpiece.
Wheels can be:
fixed or hollow
cylinders
carousels or turntables

Wheel scopes have become much more exciting with the inclusion of more pieces of different kinds and shapes of glass arranged in a variety of patterns. Allen Crandell uses over 50 different pieces of glass in the primary wheel of his scope (see page 49) and more than 150 pieces of different shapes in the second wheel. The image is breathtaking! Janice and Ray Chesnik fuse their own *millefiore* patterned pieces for some of their wheels, and use all dichroic glass in others for a gloriously brilliant display.

Spinning cylinders are a variation of traditional wheels. Some contain a small liquid-filled cylinder within a larger cylinder composed of glass, crystals, and other objects.

As the name implies, a carousel or turntable is a continuously revolving or rotating conveyor or stand on which items are placed. It can be either permanently attached to the scope or a separate piece; as simple as a tray, or as ornate as a gem-encrusted gazebo.

Size varies from a solitaire to a silo.

Materials range from alabaster to zebrawood.

Styles run the gamut from wearable to walk-in.

Shapes differ from an egg to a hot-air balloon.

Mirrors number from none to nine.

Point count in the star-like image fluctuates from 2 to 20.

The eyepiece measures from a tiny peep hole to a large binocular opening.

Objects to be viewed are limited only by the imagination.

Modes of turning the object cell go from manual to motorized.

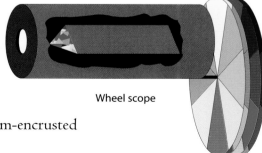

Wheel scope

4. MARBLE OR SPHERE **Single or multiple marbles are used as objects.**

Marble scope

The first marble scopes were made by attaching a small marble to a simple three-mirror system. Since the imagery was repetitious, this type soon declined in popularity. But marble scopes are new again, with several of the artists making their own marbles and using many different mirror systems. Knowing just the right combination of elements to include in these hand-blown spheres can provide extraordinary viewing. The addition of a second, third, and even fourth marble (as in the "Marbleator") increases the intricacy of the image. David Rosenfeldt recently came up with a liquid-filled marble, appropriately called "H-2-Orb."

"H-2-Orb" by David Rosenfeldt.
Photo by Allen Bryan

5. PROJECTION SCOPE **Comprises a system that projects images onto a screen or other surface.**

There are fewer projection scopes than any other type. Barbara Mitchell's SpectraSphere (see photo on page 91) is no longer in production, but there is a wonderful thirty-minute videotape of its polyangular imagery, "A Video of Kaleidoscopic Magic and Enlightenment" (Prime Lens Productions). David Fulkerson produced a limited edition of 18 "Geo" kaleidoscopes. Equipped with a small television and VCR, it turns any video into a large ever-changing kaleidoscopic sphere. By adding a second TV monitor, one can experience the excitement of viewing the original tape and projected image at the same time.

MAIN STYLES

Floor Models
Table Models
Handheld
Chairside
Sculptural
Jewelry
Miniatures
Outdoor

he body of the scope is generally structured in classic geometric shapes: cylinder, triangle, square, rectangle, and sphere. Some, however, assume the shape of a particular object, such as an airplane, train, lighthouse, birdhouse, hot-air balloon, skyscraper—virtually anything. Several artists concentrate exclusively on specialty scopes. Sam Douglas formed his acrylic scopes into replicas of the Empire State and Chrysler buildings. Marti Freund grows her own gourds, then hand paints them as beguiling animals and birds before converting them into kaleidoscopes. Greg Hanks describes the variety of hot air balloons and

Clockwise from Upper Left: Assortment of interchangeable wheels and cells. Photo by John Woodin

Lampworked pieces ("Lucinis") by Shelley Knapp

Lampworked pieces by Sherry Moser

Lampworked pieces by Marc Tickle

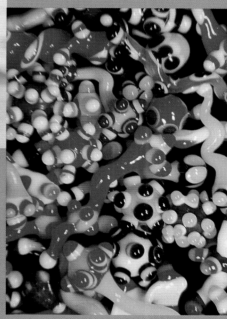

Clockwise from Upper Right:
"Fountain of Aahs", table model by
Will Smith (waterfall rotates marble)

"Acropolis" parlor scope by Ritama
Haaga. Photo by Rob Vinnedge

The "Geo" projection scope by David
Fulkerson

"Kaleidoplex," first major projection
kaleidoscope by Marshall Yaeger.
Photo by John Woodin

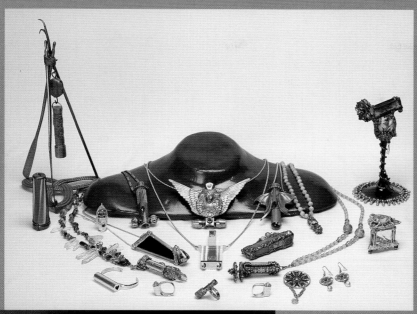

Clockwise from Upper Left:
Assortment of jewelry and minia-ture scopes. Photo by John Woodin

Ring scope with turning endpiece by Dean Krause

"Alchemist" necklaces by Will Smith

Silver necklace by Ann & Shawn Lester. Photo by Allen Bryan

Harry Winston Jewelers 18kt. gold necklace scope set with precious gems, "The Ultimate Kaleidoscope" (mirror system by Charles Karadimos). Photo by Charles Karadimos

CLockwise from Upper Left:
Hand-painted gourds made into
kaleidoscopes by Marti Freund

Greg Hanks'"Jewels in the Air" collection

Golf cart—each club is a scope—and
executive briefcase by Debra Davis

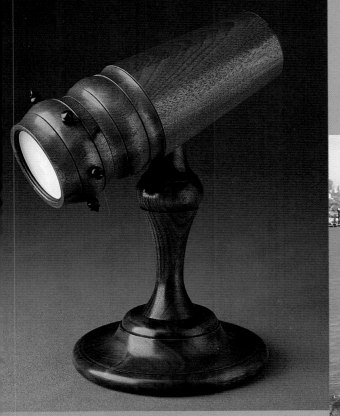

Clockwise from Upper Left:
A scarf is the object in self-lit "Muse"
by David Kalish

"Susan's Garden," a silk ribbon
embroidery scope by Sue Ross

Motorized kaleidoscope, "Captain
Nemo" by Will Smith

"Monarch I," walnut with ebony by
Glenn & Ben Straub

Clockwise from Upper Right:
"Odyssey" by Bob & Sue Rioux

Polished abalone shell scope on base
of unpolished abalone shell cradled
in deer antler by Ralph Olson. Photo
by Rich Fox

"Geotectonica" by Peggy & Steve
Kittelson. Photo by Marti Swenson

"Iridescent Dreams" by Corki Weeks

airplanes in his "Jewels in the Air Collection" as "mythical kaleidoscope airplanes designed to soar in our imagination and take us over the rainbow to our dreams." Debra Davis added to her transportation series of a school bus, mail truck, etc., such unlikely objects as a flower pot, attaché case, crayon box, and a golf bag on wheels. Timothy Krause transforms his kaleidoscopes into lighthouses (see page 14), even devising a mirror system to resemble the Fresnel lens. He will duplicate any existing lighthouse, but prefers to create ones that merely suggest a particular era.

Although floor models are extremely rare, larger kaleidoscopes are beginning to appear on the kaleidoscene. Tom Chouteau started with a "Kaleidowagon" that could hold four children. He continues to make highly unusual oversized scopes, many of which are durable enough to withstand severe weather conditions, making them appropriate for outdoor use.

To date only one chairside model has been produced—the "Bristol" (see page 21) by Wiley Jobe—but there are sure to be more, since this is one of the most user-friendly positions from which to view, and can easily be accommodated in any size domain. Handheld scopes remain the most prevalent style, due in large part to the lower cost, but also because they are easier and more comfortable to pick up and look through.

Although almost any material in the world can be used for the exterior of a kaleidoscope, glass is used more than any other, and in every conceivable form: stained, hand-blown, dichroic, fused, slumped, draped, sagged, beveled, etched, stamped, enameled, painted, Pyrex®, rods, and reverse painted.

Wood is probably the second most prevalent material. Every type and hue of exotic wood is employed for the body of the scope, from the creamiest bird's-eye maple to the richest purpleheart and the deepest ebony.

One of the most recent and unusual materials to be used for the exterior of a scope is the age-old needlework known as silk ribbon embroidery. Sue Ross has adapted this elaborate ornamental stitchery, once reserved as a fashion statement for royalty, to both the wheels and body of a new line of scopes, "Susan's Garden" (see page 57). She spends hours making bouquets and floral sprays of tiny French knots, to resemble wisteria, lilies of the valley, and other flowers, and embellishes them with equally tiny beads.

Materials

Acrylic

Alabaster

Anodized aluminum

Brass

Bronze

Ceramic

Chrome

Copper

Corian®

Cork

Fabric

Glass

Gold

Ivory

Leather

Papier-mâché

Raku

Sharkskin

Silk Ribbon Embroidery

Silver

Wood

Clockwise from Upper Right:
"Second Look" by Peter & Skeeter DeMattia (two brake rotors and steel bearings welded to a metal pipe)

Three high-tech metal kaleidoscopes by Jeff Balter (first two in a collaboration with David Meelheim)

Wood and ivory scopes—collaboration by Randy & Shelley Knapp and Paul Fletcher; Ivory tusk made into scope by Randy Knapp

"Ann" by Corki Weeks

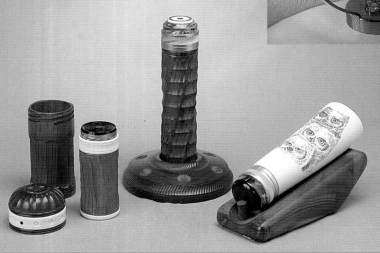

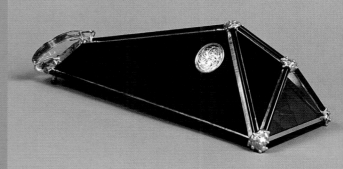

Clockwise from Upper Left:
Stamped glass mummies and scarabs on wheel scope "Eternal Collonade" by Don Ballwey

"Spikey Planet" by Marc Tickle

"Spheara" by Sherry Moser

"Crystal Pillar" by Bob & Grace Ade

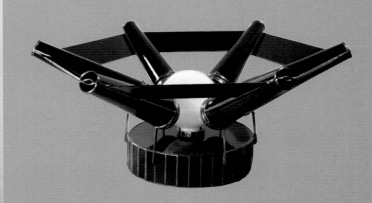

Clockwise from Upper Left:
"Hummingbird" by Bob & Sue Rioux.
See image on page 75

"Party time(s) six" by Charles Karadimos

Reverse painting on glass scopes by
Marc Tickle

"Talisman" by Peggy & Steve Kittelson.
Photo by Marti Swenson

Musical wheel scope, dichroic glass plate,
hand-blown marble scope and marbles
by David & Debbie Rosenfeldt. Photo by
Allen Bryan

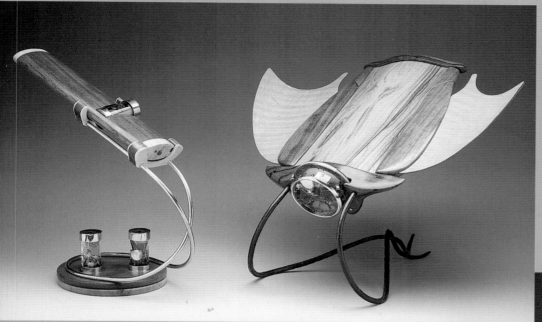

Clockwise from Upper Left:
"Cordalee Launched" and "Manta Ray" by Henry Bergeson. Photo by Priscilla Montoya

From Alabaster (Ben Ansley) to Zebra Wood (Randy & Shelley Knapp). Photo by John Woodin

"High Roller" by Janice & Ray Chesnik. Photo by Don Darrock

VARIETY OF INTERIOR IMAGES

Interchanging colors meld and merge • capricious patterns shift and fuse • vanishing . . . . only to reappear • rewoven from an earlier web • new beauty and symetry . . . over and over again

The heart or soul of the kaleidoscope is its mirrors. They reveal the hidden beauty and symmetry of each unfolding image. Scope artist John Culver relates an old parable about mirrors: "They say if you hold a clear glass in front of yourself, you see the world through it, but if you take that piece of glass and put a thin veneer of silver (money) on it, then all you see is yourself. This relates especially to kaleidoscopes . . . they transform mirrors that reflect your image into mirrors that see inside yourself."

Ordinary mirrors are not suitable for quality scopes because they do not provide clear, sharp reflections. First or front-surface mirrors that have a reflective coating on their front surface are essential for quality imagery. Light reflects only once from such a mirror, which gives a sharper image. Regular mirrors are coated on the rear surface, so light is reflected twice—once off the mirror and once off the image itself, leaving the edges of the image fuzzy.

Opposite Top: Tapered three-mirror spherical image of the American flag photographed by Joe Polevoi through the Geoscope by Prism Designs

Opposite Bottom: A tapered four-mirror spherical image from tenth anniversary Brewster Society Commemorative scope by Margaret Neher. Photo by Dan Robinson

Image from a two-mirror system

Right: Image from a three-mirror system

The shape and dimension of the image are determined by the number and position of the mirrors and the angles at which they are placed. The colors and patterns are dictated by the objects viewed.

While new, complicated systems are being developed even as this book goes to press, there are basically two major mirror systems that have been used in kaleidoscopes since their invention in 1816: the two-mirror, which produces one central image, and the three-mirror, which produces reflected images throughout the entire field of view. Both are set up in a triangular configuration in a tube, much like a prism.

In the two-mirror system, the two mirrors are arranged in a "V" with the third side of the triangle a blackened or non-reflective surface. The angle of the "V" determines the number of reflections. The closer the angle between the mirrors, the more reflected images, and thus the more intricate the pattern. The most perfect symmetry and best image result when the angle between the mirrors divides equally into 360 degrees.

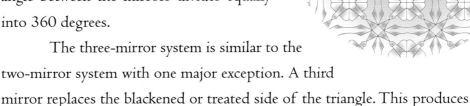

The three-mirror system is similar to the two-mirror system with one major exception. A third mirror replaces the blackened or treated side of the triangle. This produces

60°: 6-fold symmetry–
3-point star by Paretti

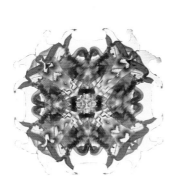

45°: 8-fold symmetry–
4-point star by Jobe

36°: 10-fold symmetry–
5-point star by Knapps

30°: 12-fold symmetry–
6-point star by Karadimos

continuous honeycomb-like patterns throughout the entire field of view. The 60°-60°-60° equilateral triangle is the most common construction and produces the simplest of the repetitive patterns. The 45°-45°-90° gives a more complex symmetry as it combines merging triangular and square shapes. But probably the most interesting image produced by the three-mirror system is the 30°-60°-90°. The symmetry of this latter type is fourfold (from the 90° angle), sixfold (from the 60° angle), and 12-fold (from the 30° angle).

Other systems give distinctive results: A square four-mirror arrangement, for example, produces repeated square patterns, while a four-mirror rectangular arrangement produces repeated rectangular patterns. The images created are striped patterns, since the reflections move directionally up-down, and right-left. Several variations of these four-mirror systems provide different images, including the "Chorus Line" originated by Corki Weeks and the "Gemini," first introduced by Sheryl Koch.

Tapered three- or four-mirror systems produce the illusion of a spherical three-dimensional image. Cylindrical tubes lined with a reflective material will produce a spiraling effect. Since there are no angles involved in this style, the reflection seems to climb through the tube asymmetrically.

Computer-generated images by Charles Karadimos

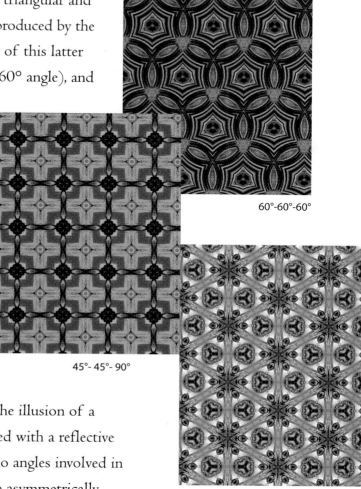

60°-60°-60°

45°- 45°- 90°

30°- 60°- 90°

22.5°: 16-fold symmetry–
8-point star by Karadimos

20°:18-fold symmetry–
9-point star by Straub

18°: 20-fold symmetry–
10-point star by Raredon

15°: 24-fold symmetry–
12-point star by Karadimos

Right: Four-mirror image by Ray &
Janice Chesnik. Photo by Don Darrock

Variations of retangular images from
"Brocade" and "Iris" by Peggy & Steve
Kittelson. Photos by Marti Swenson

"Gemini" by Sheryl Koch. Photo by
Janice Chesnick

"Aurora" image by Luc & Sallie Durette

The polyangular system is an elaborate variation of the two-mirror configuration, in which one or both of the mirrors can be adjusted, changing the angle of the "V," and thus the number of symmetrical reflections. This is the ultimate and most satisfying arrangement of any, but also the most difficult to construct, and only a few artists have attempted it since Brewster's accomplishment in 1816. The first contemporary use of the polyangular system was in Barbara Mitchell's "SpectraSphere"—a projection scope. Then Willie Stevenson introduced both a parlor and handheld model. Wiley Jobe feels it is the only system, and builds it into every one of his beautiful wood scopes: chairside, floor, table, and handheld.

"Quintette" by Janice and Ray Chesnik. Photo by Don Darrock

Some artists place two or more different mirror systems into one instrument. "Quintette" by Janice and Ray Chesnik contains five separate systems. But multidimensional, rather than numerical, is the direction imagery is taking today.

While the exterior of the kaleidoscope has been in a continuous state of transformation ever since its invention, it is only recently that the mirror structure and format have been changed. Mirror systems of high complexity are being researched and developed that display three-dimensional forms. These complex mirror arrangements, subject to infinite possibilities, render the interior itself as sculptural as the exterior.

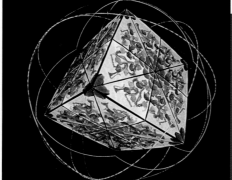

Cube from "Picasso's Dream"

Dodecahedron from "Pandora's Box"

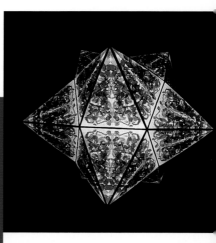

Star Dodecahedron from "Starlite"

The seven images below are examples of new complex polyhedral shapes photographed through scopes by Don Doak.

OBJECTS DETERMINE COLOR AND PATTERN

The colors and patterns of each image are a result of the objects that are placed at the end of the mirror system. Even ugly things become beautiful when viewed through a complex mirror system. But the prettier the object, the more varied the shape and texture, and the more harmonious the balance of color, the more exciting the image.

Glass pieces, especially lampworked shapes, are the objects used most frequently in cells. They give even more sparkle (especially dichroic glass) than genuine gemstones. But it is "found objects" that bring the imagination to life more than anything. Carmen Colley was among the first to use found objects in both the wheels and the body of her scopes. In one large ornate parlor scope she used such unlikely items as cicada wings, cat whiskers, coffee crystals, coriander, a snake's rattle, moth antennae, and live scarabaeid beetles! The latter isn't as outlandish as it might seem at first, since Brewster himself suggested

Objects Used in Cells

Beads

Dichroic glass

Dried flowers

Feathers

Fish

Found objects

Gemstones

Glass-stamped pieces

Jewels

Lampworked glass pieces

Liquid-filled ampules

Plastic baubbles and glitter

Polarized filters

Rocks

Scarves

Seashells

Silk ribbon embroidery

Soap bubbles

Water fountain

and on and on

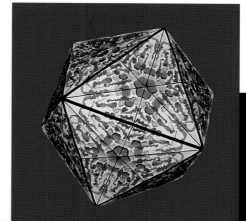

Imploding Dodecahedron, from "Living Lantern"

Above: Icosahedron from "Plato's No Jive Five"

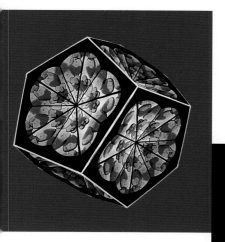

Right: Star Icosahedron from "Plato's No Jive Five"

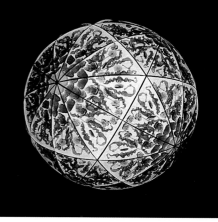

Pure Sphere from "Spherical Aspirations"

in his original treatise that the insertion of a live insect into the object case would add interest. Andrew Leary's idea to use bubbles as the object in his parlor scope also may have been influenced by Brewster. One of the last articles Brewster prepared for publication was on the subject of soap bubbles.

Many consider liquid-filled ampules with air bubbles the ultimate

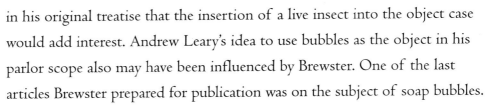

objects for viewing. They give the most intriguing optical display, as movement continues even after the scope is at rest. For many years Bill O'Connor was the only glass blower to master this skill since Bush. He is still considered by many to be the dean of this form, although several other artists, including Ben Straub, Shantidevi, Marc Tickle, and Sherry Moser, are becoming adept; no doubt many more will.

Liquid-filled ampules in bell jar by Bill O'Connor

Liquid-filled vessels by Sherry Moser

PHOTOGRAPHING KALEIDOSCOPE IMAGES

Photographing images through a kaleidoscope is different from photographing kaleidoscopic imagery of people, places, and things. For many years it was difficult for an amateur photographer to take good photos of kaleidoscope images, mainly because the eyepieces were so small. Then artists began enlarging the eyepiece, making photography much easier. There is no special lens required to shoot an interior image through a kaleidoscope. In order to achieve proper focus, it is necessary to match the focal length of the lens on the camera to the distance between the eye and the image.

There are two devices available to create kaleidoscopic photographs of the surrounding world: the C. Bennett "ScopeLens," which can be attached to almost any 35mm camera, and the Reynolds "Camerascope" by Kaleidovisions, which fits any standard camera. Joe Polevoi used both of these to get the stunning photographs pictured on pages 35 and 37.

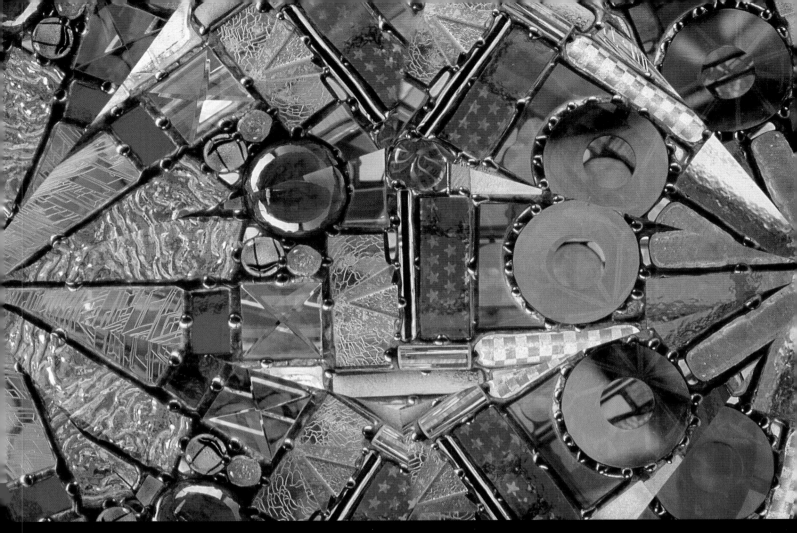

Interior image of "Hummingbird"
scope by Sue & Bob Rioux

"Jubiliation Series" by David Sugich

Images by Randy & Shelley Knapp

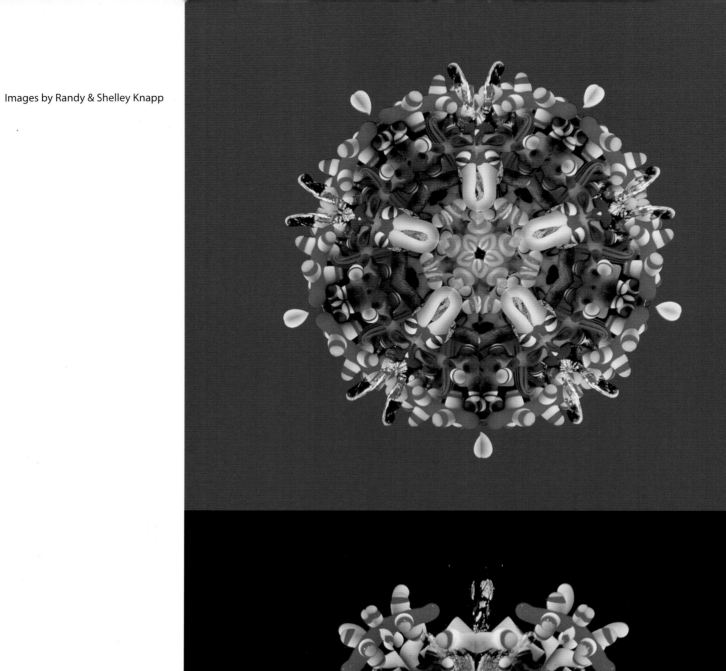
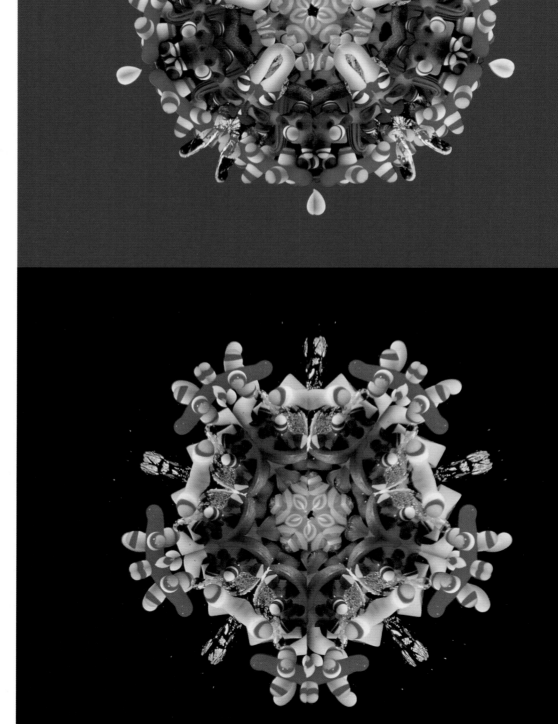

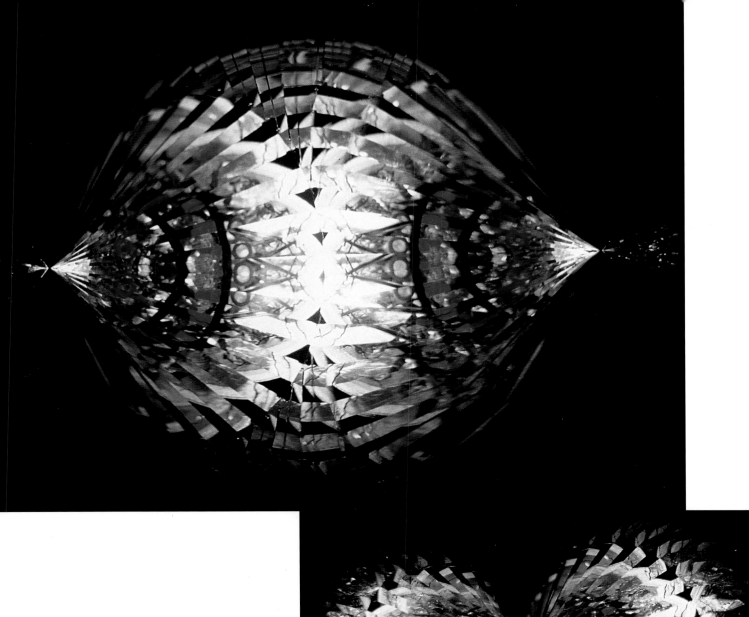

Experimental images by Sam Douglas

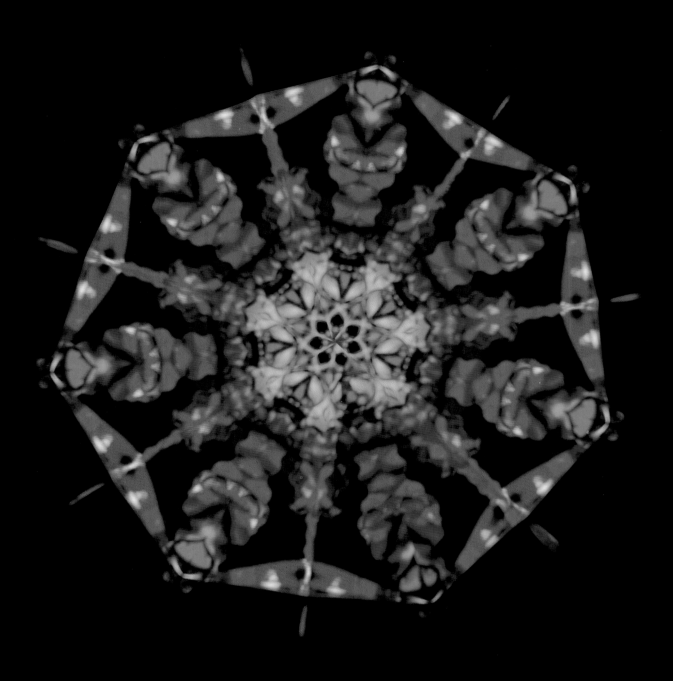

"Firedance" by Luc & Sallie Durette

"Shadowdance" by Luc & Sallie Durette

"O'Tannenbaum" by Luc & Sallie Durette

"The Rose Scope" by Steve & Peggy
Kittelson. Photo by Marti Swenson

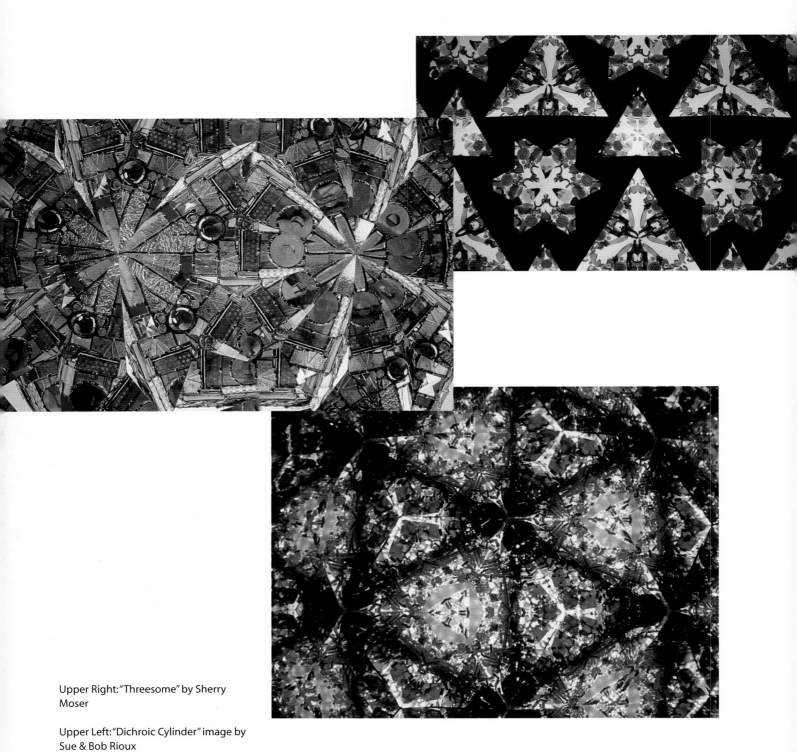

Upper Right: "Threesome" by Sherry Moser

Upper Left: "Dichroic Cylinder" image by Sue & Bob Rioux

Lower Right: Three-mirror equilaterial system in "Garnet Firefly" by Greg Hanks

"Chandala" image by Sherry Moser

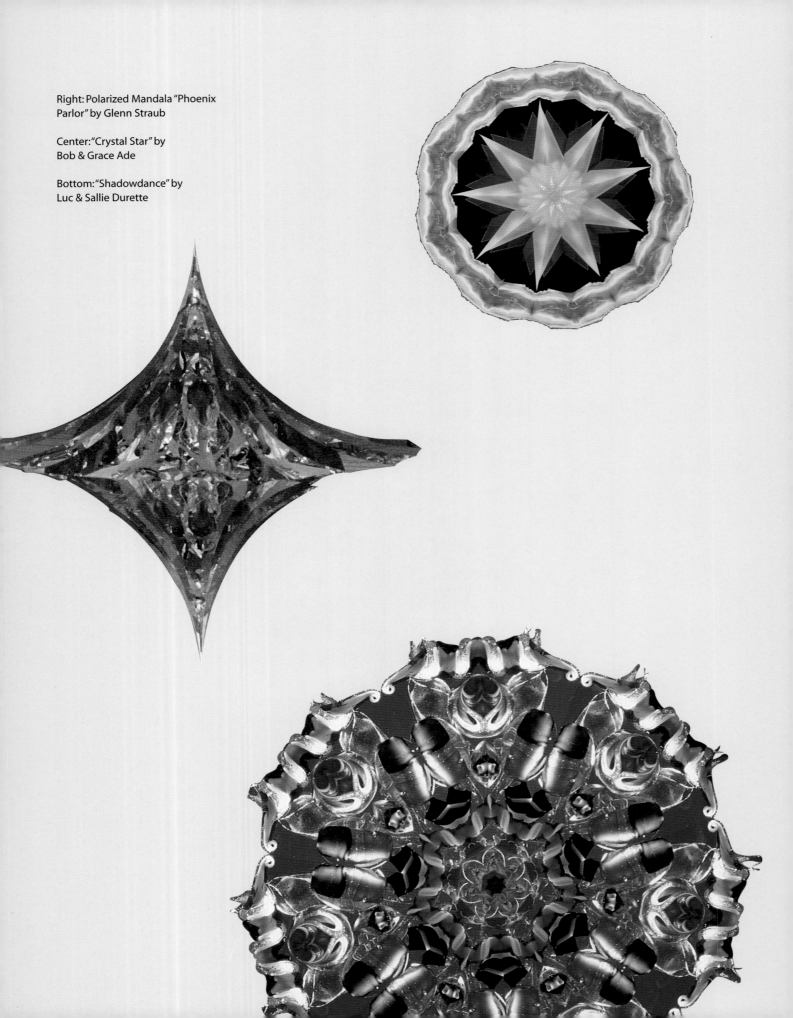

Right: Polarized Mandala "Phoenix Parlor" by Glenn Straub

Center: "Crystal Star" by Bob & Grace Ade

Bottom: "Shadowdance" by Luc & Sallie Durette

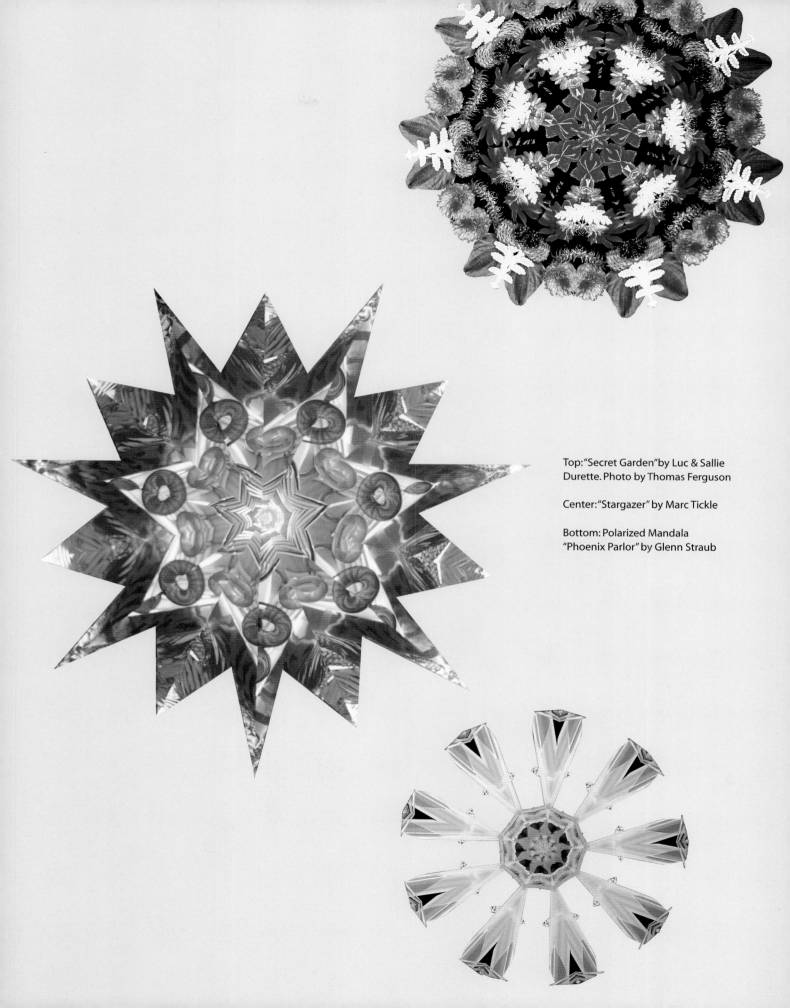

Top: "Secret Garden" by Luc & Sallie
Durette. Photo by Thomas Ferguson

Center: "Stargazer" by Marc Tickle

Bottom: Polarized Mandala
"Phoenix Parlor" by Glenn Straub

AWARD WINNERS

The kaleidoscope acts as a spiritual battery · continually recharging the spirit · transforming imagination and energizing creativity ·

. . . and the envelope please

The Brewster Society Award for Creative Ingenuity is not simply an automatic annual presentation. It is reserved for the creation of a scope that initiates a completely new feature or concept. **Corki Weeks** was the first recipient in 1986 for her unprecedented idea of housing two different mirror systems (both a three-mirror and a two-mirror) in the same instrument.

Barbara Mitchell received the second award in 1987 for her "SpectraSphere"—a rear-projection polyangular kaleidoscope (the angles of the mirrors can be changed). The SpectraSphere can accommodate any type cell (dry-tumbling, oil-filled, hand-painted, transparencies, or polarizing filters). It can be projected on any size screen, and is equally suited to be viewed on an individual plexiglass hemisphere.

Opposite Left: Corki Weeks
Opposite Right: Barbara Mitchell operating her "SpectraSphere." Photo by Joel Riner

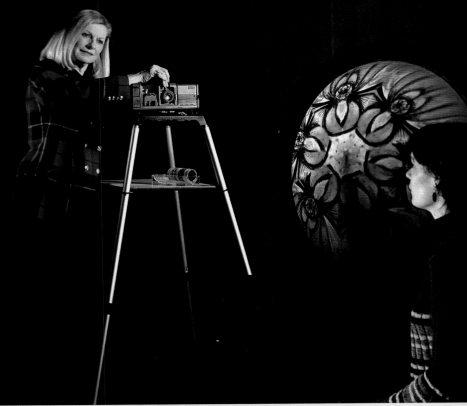

Photo by John Woodin

In 1989, **Willie Stevenson's** "Whatever Blows Your Skirt Up" (re-named "Whatever Tilts Your Kilt" to add a wee bit of Scottish flavor) won for the still unduplicated concept of an automatically motorized polyangular system. The object case of this large floor model contains hand-painted silk scarves that, blown about by a fan, dance in perfect rhythm to music delivered from a hidden cassette player.

Sherry Moser was the first to treat and utilize the mirrors as an integral part of the image. Her "Journey" in 1991 was the fourth winner of the Award for Creative Ingenuity.

In 1992 the fifth award went to **Don Doak**, who applied Buckminster Fuller's geodesic math principles in the assembly of multiple groups of tapered mirrors and came up with the "KaleidoSphere." This is a scope you look at rather than into; the illusion remains constant, whether you are standing or moving.

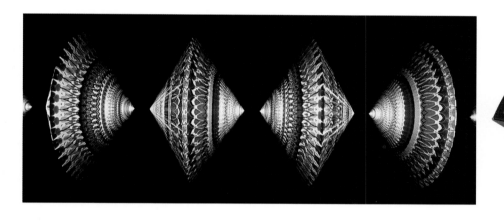

In 1993, the honor was given to **Steven Gray** for his cumulative conceptual contributions, rather than for one particular piece. Nearly a dozen major works combine Steven's matchless woodworking skill with his unparalleled mirror configurations.

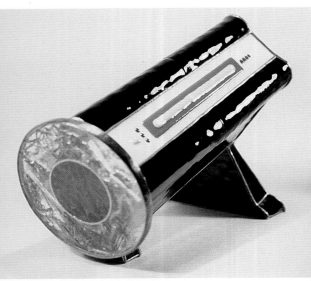

Charles Karadimos won for his unique parlor scope "Tessera" (1994). Viewed with both eyes, four completely distinct and separate images can be seen in the same field, while the object chamber generates a radically different color scheme at each image point.

"The Monet Gallery" (1995) was a collaboration by **Sherry Moser** and **Judith Paul**. The interior image actually replicates the exterior painting (Judith's interpretation of Monet's water lilies) complete with lampworked water lilies and a hand-painted Japanese bridge. This artistic innovation is presented on a gold-toned easel, and the viewer is treated to a continually changing Monet-style painting in a narrow rectangular gold frame.

Photos by Robert Switzer

Randy Knapp won for the "Marbleator" in 1997. This "high-tech" metal floor model resembles a pin-ball machine or nickelodeon. Four of the 55 hand-blown marbles, propelled through two separate mirror systems by an elevator, can be viewed at the same time as push buttons operate flashing lights and colors!

Carol and Tom Paretti's "Feather & Leather" was another winner in 1997—for the ingenious concept of turning (or blowing) beautifully colored feathers by means of a perfume atomizer.

In 1997 "Pandora's Box," **Don Doak** opened an unexplored area in which there exist infinite possibilities for the evolution of yet unperceived 3-D images to evolve. The image in this scope is a star dodecahedron.

Photo by Robert Vigiletti

In 1998, a new category was added. **Carolyn Bennett** was the first to receive the Special Achievement Award for her continuing contributions of merit that advance and enrich every facet of the kaleidoscope renaissance.

Photo by Lee Widder

eople's Choice Awards were presented in various categories at many of the annual Brewster Society conventions. The winners:

1993	Louisville	Favorite Kaleidoscope	**"Fanta Sea" by Luc & Sallie Durette**
1994	San Francisco	Three-way tie:	**"Sphere" by Charles Karadimos**
			"Brainstorm" by Don Doak
			"Circle of Friends" by Sherry Moser
1995	Chicago	Limited Edition, Best Image	**"Pandora's Box" by Don Doak**
		Limited Edition, Best Exterior	**"The Monet Gallery" by Sherry Moser & Judith Paul**
		Production Scope, Best Image	**"Sundog" by Randy & Shelley Knapp**
		Production Scope, Best Exterior	**"Magnolia in Bloom" by Peggy & Steve Kittelson**
1996	Corning, N.Y.	Best Limited Edition	**"Sea Angel" by Sue & Bob Rioux**
		Best Non-Limited Edition	**"Wishes" by Sherry Moser**
		Most Innovative	**"On the Threshold of a Dream" by Luc & Sallie Durette**
1998	Orlando, Florida	Best Image	**"Fibonacci" by Marc Tickle**
		Rookie Award	**"Sport-o-scope" by 10-yr.-old Alex Rioux**
		Oh Wow! Award	**"Fireworks" Kaleidoscope™ by Kaesana Inc.**

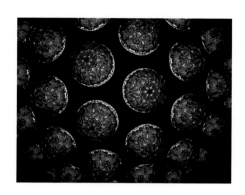

Image from "On the Threshold of a Dream"

"Fanta Sea"

Luc & Sallie Durette with son Noah

Clockwise from Upper Left:
"Circle of Friends," "Sphere," image
from "Brainstorm," Peggy & Steve
Kittelson, "Magnolia in Bloom"

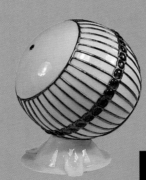

Photos by Marti Swenson

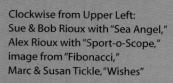

Clockwise from Upper Left:
Sue & Bob Rioux with "Sea Angel,"
Alex Rioux with "Sport-o-Scope,"
image from "Fibonacci,"
Marc & Susan Tickle, "Wishes"

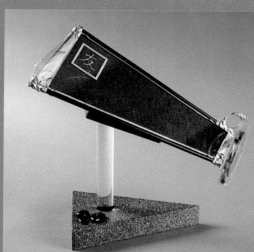

"Fireworks." Photo by Jacob Wong

Kaesana Inc.: Jim Hirsch, Margaret
& Mark Eilrich, Jason Wong, Peggy
& Steve Kittelson

There are two categories that, while not designated for an award, do merit honorable mention. Kaleidoscope artist/composer David Sugich wrote a musical tribute to the kaleidoscope that the Brewster Society has adopted as its official anthem. At the opening of each annual convention, David accompanies himself on the guitar as he sings the meaningful words of his mellifluous composition, "Kaleidoscope."

Photo of artist by Brenda Barrett

The other category deserving singular recognition involves photography. Capturing well-focused photographs of intricate kaleidoscope imagery is a prized skill in itself. Light sculptor Adam Peiperl stands out as the one person who consistently achieves exacting, sharp, and accurate renditions of kaleidoscope images as illustrated by each chapter opening photograph in this book. Peiperl has also mastered his own optical technique for photographically interpreting the real world around him of people, places, and things in novel kaleidoscopic patterns as exemplified here by his photograph of the Eiffel Tower.

Photo © Adam Peiperl/TSM 1995

GALLERIES, MUSEUMS, AND SHOPS

Kaleidoscopes express a universal celebration of happiness •

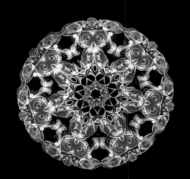

and "Wow" is the verbal burst of applause worldwide

The "Cozy Scope Salon" redefines the concept of a museum. In 1997, Cozy Baker converted her home into a house-museum for the exclusive benefit of Brewster Society members. It is the only place in the world with every type and style of kaleidoscope under one roof, from an original Brewster to the very newest scopes. In addition to several rooms filled with hundreds of hands-on scopes, there is a library containing books, periodicals, newspaper articles, videotapes, and photographs pertaining to the subject. A dark room permits special showings of Barbara Mitchells's "SpectraSphere," Marshall Yaeger's "Kaleidoplex," and other important projection scopes.

The "Cozy Scope Salon" is also home of the kaleidoscope billed for many years as the world's largest. Actually, this 500 pound, 12-foot long, 6-foot high scope, built by Al Brickel in the early 1970s, is still the largest known conventional hand-manipulated type (noncomputerized), though it has been

Opposite: Solarium in the Cozy Baker Salon. Photo by John Woodin

Miniature replica of Cozy Baker's living room by stained glass artist Carl Goeller. Tiny scopes by originating artists.

Living Room of the Cozy Baker Scope Salon. Photo by John Woodin

Kaleidoscope mailbox

Opposite: KaleidAquarium and image by Tom & Sherry Rupert. Photos by John Woodin

"Fountain of Aahs" by Will Smith, floor model (waterfall rotates object marble)

eclipsed as the largest scope of any kind. Other large one-of-a-kind scopes on display are "Martian Garden" by Tom Chouteau, which children can climb on and peer into, and "KaleidAquarium" by Sherry and Tom Rupert, in which the fish are the swimming objects.

From a kaleidoscope mailbox at the entrance of the property to a water fountain kaleido-sculpture (Fountain of Aahs) at the front door, and stained glass windows of scope images, privileged Brewster Society members can enjoy a total and enriching kaleidoscope experience.

Strathmore Hall Arts Center in Bethesda, Maryland, was the site of the first kaleidoscope exhibition in the United States in September 1985. Its popularity and success led to several other exhibitions over the years, and Strathmore was also the first major art center to maintain a permanent exhibit of kaleidoscopes. A special cabinet was built to showcase examples of both antique and contemporary kaleidoscopes from the Cozy Baker collection.

Former largest kaleidoscope in the world by Al Brickel. Photo by John Woodin

Opposite: Cabinet at Strathmore Hall Arts Center with kaleidoscopes from the Cozy Baker collection. Photo by Gary Landsman

COZY BAKER
KALEIDOSCOPE CENTER

The KALEIDOSCOPE
BOOK and KIT

In 1996, kaleidoscopes soared to a new height (60 feet) with the Kaatskill Kaleidoscope in Mt. Tremper, New York. Entrepreneur Dean Gitter converted a silo into a kaleidoscope that is certified by the *Guiness Book of World Records* as the world's largest scope. Kaleidoscope artist Charles Karadimos designed the 38-foot mirror system, using a new lightweight reflective material. A computerized show set to music is projected onto a giant sphere with an apparent 50 foot radius. New kaleidoscopic attractions are continually added to the Kaleidoworld at Catskill Corners, including "The Amazing Dondoakahedron," billed as the world's second-largest kaleidoscope.

Computer print of the world's largest kaleidoscope at Catskill Corners

Although the kaleidoscope's communication is nonverbal and viewing is a private experience, let two or more collectors get together with an assortment of scopes and communication gets quite vocal and the viewing becomes a group event. David Meelheim of Stardust in McLean, Virginia, says he can't think of any other item that prompts cus-

"Psychescope" by Tom Chouteau in the Kaleidoworld at Catskill Corners

Waterwheel fountain kaleidoscope by Tom Chouteau in the Kaleidoworld at Catskill Corners

tomers who were previously total strangers into exchanging comments and sharing "views"—even extending invitations to see one another's collections.

One of a handful of early shops specializing in kaleidoscopes, Stardust has always looked for innovative ways to bring collectors and collections together. While early exhibits were successful, only a limited number were able to view them first-hand. Later, a full-color catalogue enabled greater numbers to enjoy the tremendous variety of designs available. But to truly appreciate the kaleidoscope's enchantment, a hands-on experience is necessary. With this in mind, Stardust is launching the "Scopemobile"—a specially outfitted vehicle that will travel the country bringing the latest in kaleidoscopes to America's front door. Retired pieces, antique, and toy scopes will be on display, and informational videos will round out the educational end of this storefront-on-wheels.

Hand of the Craftsman in Nyack, NY

Jan and Shel Haber, owners of Hand of the Craftsman in Nyack, New York, were among the very first to add kaleidoscopes to their inventory of fine crafts. They were also the first to feature an annual scope festival each spring and fall. Jan says, "There seems to be something inherent in kaleidoscopes that prompts a desire to share—both verbally and optically. We have watched many strong friendships develop over the years among our scope customers, including a romance that started at our kaleido-bar. And they do more to perk folks up than anything. We've seen smiles replace stress lines on many a harried shopper."

Nellie Bly in Jerome, AZ. Photo by Margaret M. Hinrichsen

Eric Sinizer first put kaleidoscopes in his San Francisco shop, Light Opera Gallery, mainly for his own enjoyment. He soon realized their potential, and was the first to include scopes as a major item in his shop of fine glass and Russian lacquer boxes. He also published the first catalog of kaleidoscopes.

Mary Wills keeps almost as many kaleidoscopes in her home (153 in her bathroom alone) as in her shop, Nellie Bly. Located in the tiny hill-town of Jerome, Arizona, this fascinating shop boasts a large well-lit kaleidoscope bar. Mary assures customers that in addition to making appropriate gifts for

every occasion, kaleidoscopes are ideal for all interior decorating needs as they complement every motif and any period for either the home or office.

The Woods, newest Davlins store in Minneapolis, MN. Photo by Melani Weber

Tedde Ready feels a heart and soul connection with kaleidoscopes and has been selling them since the early 1980s. She shares her enthusiasm and passion for scopes with customers in her Cambria, California shop called A Different Point of View. Referring to scopes as "soul food," Tedde advocates using them each day to "massage the spirit and refresh the heart."

In addition to selling kaleidoscopes in all four of their Davlins stores in Minneapolis, Minnesota, Dave and Linda Looney present an annual exhibition, circulate a scope newsletter, and maintain a web site on the Internet.

Eileen Kremen has had more kaleidoscope exhibitions (19 so far) than any other single gallery. She presents a two-month exhibit twice a year in her Fullerton, California, gallery. This means that one third of each year is devoted to a kaleidoscope celebration.

In Boston, Whippoorwill Crafts was so successful in its Faneuil Hall location that Karen and Bob Hohler opened a second store in the Prudential Center. "For years we have been impressed with the kaleidoscope community," Karen remarks, "for its genuine openness and sharing. In my experience, there is no group in the craft world like it. These characteristics have contributed to the success of the kaleidoscope renaissance and the Brewster Society."

Whippoorwill Crafts in Boston. Photo by Roger Ide

Opposite: Kaleidoscopes in Mary Wills' bathroom. Photo by Margaret M. Hinrichsen

Kaleidoscopes are displayed in every nook and corner of the foyer, sitting rooms, parlors, dining room, and gift shop at the Veranda, a delightful bed and breakfast in Senoia, Georgia. Antique scopes and contemporary models grace mantels and sideboards. Guest bedrooms are named for particular scopes they contain, and tiny scopes replace candy each night as the bedtime pillow treat.

David Wallace, owner of After the Rain in New York City, definitely views kaleidoscopes as more than objects to sell. "I don't claim kaleidoscopes will save us, heal the planet, or solve racial injustice . . . [but] they remind us that in our deepest selves lies the desire for beauty and harmony."

After the Rain in New York City

Sun Country Kaleidoscopes in Carmel, California has been a showcase for American-designed kaleidoscopes since 1985. It is owned and operated by marble artist Ray Anderson and his wife Diane. Collectors themselves, Ray and Diane have created a veritable treasure box "where the pines meet the sea." Although a tiny shop, it boasts an extensive, ever-changing collection of scopes by major artists, and always a few by collectors-turned-artists, whom the Andersons encourage.

Pat Branda and Pat Asay are having great fun and success in a shop that sells only kaleidoscopes. La Casita de Kaleidoscopes is part of one of the oldest buildings in the Historic Old Town section of Albuquerque, New Mexico. Visitors from all over the world enjoy this atmospheric shop with its antique furniture and display cabinets chock-full of exciting kaleidoscopes.

Sun Country in Carmel, CA. Photo by Diane Dobrante

La Casita de Kaleidoscopes in Albuquerque, NM

Although the kaleidoscope renaissance is an American phenomenon, interest in scopes is slowly growing in other countries. Kaleidoscope Mukashi-Kan opened in Tokyo in 1995 as Japan's first gallery devoted entirely to kaleidoscopes. Owner Michi Araki also launched a Japanese chapter of the Brewster Society in 1998. When Paul Kustow introduced kaleidoscopes to his clients at The Alexander Collections in Amersham Old Town, Bucks, England, the response was enthusiastic. He is also importing and distributing kaleidoscopes to retailers throughout the United Kingdom.

Dr. Hirotomo Ochi, chairman of Nikken Foods Company, Ltd., is planning the world's first major kaleidoscope art museum to open in Japan early in the new century. The Teruko Tsuji Memorial Art Museum will be located in Sendei, about two hours by train north of Tokyo. The main building of the museum will be divided into four wings, symbolic of the four seasons. Outside gardens with a waterfall, moss-covered steps, alleys, and bridges, will enhance the artistic milieu of ornamental trees and foliage. In addition to spacious exhibit areas, there will be a kaleidoscope art-therapy room with comfortable seating, and a fountain reservoir with flower beds for viewing through several large scopes. From a rotating ceiling kaleidoscope to a mosaic tile floor, visitors will be surrounded by kaleidoscopes of every size, shape, and description, including some of the world's greatest and most important.

Architectural drawing of Teruko Tsuji Memorial Art Museum in Japan

The following is a compilation of galleries/shops that have been featuring kaleidoscopes since the early 1980s, plus a few newer additions that specialize in these wonders.

Image from "Tripos" by Charles Karadimos

ARIZONA

Nellie Bly (Mary Wills)
136 Main Street
Jerome 86331
(520) 634-02

Out of Hand
(Karen and Bob Klein)
6166 N. Scottsdale Road (The Borgata) Scottsdale 85250
(602) 998-0977

ARKANSAS

KaleidoKites
(Linda and Steve Rogers)
No. 1C Spring Street
Eureka Springs 72632
(501) 253-6596

CALIFORNIA

Eileen Kremen Gallery
(Eileen and Harris Kremen)
619 N. Harbor Blvd.
Fullerton 92632
(714) 879-1391

Light Opera Gallery
(Eric Sinizer)
460 Post St.
San Francisco 94102
(800) 553-4800

A Different Point of View
(Tedde Ready)
777 Main St.
Cambria 93428
(805) 927-4742

Sun Country
(Ray and Diane Anderson)
Ocean & San Carlos
Carmel 93921
(408) 625-5907

COLORADO

J. Fenton Gallery
(Joan Fenton)
100 Elbert Lane
Snowmass Village 81615
(970) 923-5457

FLORIDA

Fusion
(Coleen and John Allcorn)
121 E. Tarpon Ave.
Tarpon Springs 34689
(813) 934-9396

ILLINOIS

The Artists' Works
(Judy Kaponya)
32 W. Chicago Ave.
Naperville 60540
(630) 357-3774

Off-the-Hoof
(Susan and Gerry Morris)
2100 Central Street
Evanston 60201
(800) SCOPE-18

IOWA

The Plant Ranch
(Karl and Jean Schilling)
Highway 65 and 9
Manley 50456
(888) 454-2068

KENTUCKY

Ky Center for the Arts
(Karen Townsend)
5 Riverfront Plaza
Louisville 40202
(502) 562-0165

MARYLAND

Easy Street
(Marcia and Terry Moore)
7 Frances Street
Annapolis 21401
(410) 263-5556

Strathmore Hall Arts Center Gift Shop (Charleen McClellan)
10701 Rockville Pike
N. Bethesda 20852
(301) 530-0540

MASSACHUSETTS

Impulse (Sonny Bayer)
188 Commercial Street
Provincetown 02657
(508) 487-1154

Whippoorwill Crafts
(Karen and Bob Hohler)
126 S. Market, Faneuil Hall
Boston 02109
(617) 523-5149
and 800 Boylston Street,
Prudential Center
02118
(617) 236-2050

MINNESOTA

Davlins
(David and Linda Looney)
2028 Burnsville Center
Burnsville 55337
(612) 892-3665
and 2652 Southdale Center,
6601 France Ave. S.
Edina 55435
(612) 926-6838
and 116 Rosedale Center
Roseville 55113
(612) 631-2162
and The Woods at Maple Grove
(612) 416-WOOD

The Glass Scope
(Karl and Jean Schilling)
314 Main Street,
Riverfront Centre
Red Wing 55066
(651) 388-2048

NEVADA

Paper & Gold
(Richard Erickson)
Caesar's Tahoe
Stateline 89449
(702) 588-4438

NEW JERSEY

A Mano (Ana Leyland)
36 N. Union Street
Lambertville 08530
(609) 397-0063

NEW MEXICO

La Casita de Kaleidoscopes
(Pat Asay and Pat Branda)
206 1/2 San Felipe NW, #7 1/2
Patio Market
Albuquerque 87104
(505) 247-4242

NEW YORK

After the Rain (David Wallace)
149 Mercer Street
New York 10012
(212) 431-1044

Kaatskill Kaleidostore
(Dean and Lynn Gitter)
Rt. 28 Mt. Pleasant 12457
(914) 688-9700

Craft Company #6
(Lynn Allinger and Gary Stam)
785 University Ave.
Rochester 14607
(716) 473-3413

The Glass Menagerie
(Jackie and Dick Pope)
37 East Market Street
Corning 14830
(607) 962-6300

Hand of the Craftsman
(Jan and Shel Haber)
52 S. Broadway
Nyack 10960
(914) 358-6622

NORTH CAROLINA

New Morning Gallery
(John Cram)
7 Boston Way
Asheville 28803
(828) 274-2831

PENNSYLVANIA

A Mano (Ana Leyland)
128 S. Main Street
New Hope 18938
(215) 862-5122

Mykonos (Barbara Robbins)
Glen Eagle Square, R. 202
Chadds Ford 19317
(610) 558-8000

Wood You Believe
(Glenn Straub)
The Artworks at Doneckers
100 State Street, Studio 126
Ephrata 17522
(717) 738-9595

TEXAS

Free Flight Gallery
(Sandy and Ed Smith)
Galleria Mall, Suite 2390
13350 Dallas Parkway
Dallas 75240
(972) 701-9566
and Westend Marketplace
603 Munger Suite 309
Dallas 75202
(972) 720-9147

VERMONT

The Unicorn (Jeffrey Kahn)
15 Central Street
Woodstock 05091
(802) 457-2480

Shimmering Glass
(Stephen Fishman)
Rt. 100
Waterbury 05676
(802) 244-8134
and **Stowe Craft Gallery**
Mountain Rd.
Stowe 05672
(802) 253-4693

VIRGINIA

J. Fenton Gallery
(Joan Fenton)
110 S. Henry Street
Williamsburg 23185
(757) 221-8200

Quilts Unlimited
(Joan Fenton)
1051 Millmont
Charlottesville 22903
(804) 979-8110

**Stardust catalog and
Scopemobile**
(David Meelheim)
Mc Lean
(800) 272-6731

WASHINGTON, D.C. AREA

Appalachian Springs
(David and Polly Brooks)
1415 Wisconsin Ave. 20007
(202) 337-5780
and Union Station 50
Massachusetts Ave. NE 20002
(202) 682-0505
and Reston Town Center,
11877 Market Street
Reston VA 22090
(703) 478-2218
and 1041 Rockville Pike
Rockville MD 20850
(301) 230-1380

INTERNATIONAL
ENGLAND

The Alexander Collections
(Paul Kustow)
No. 1 The Broadway
Amersham Old Town, Bucks
HP7 01L
Fax: 011-44-149-443-4661

JAPAN

Kaleidoscope Mukashi-Kan
(Michi Araki)
2-13-8 Azabujyuban, Minato-ku
Tokyo 106
Fax: 011-81-33-453-4439

Seishido Myers Ltd.
(Tomie Imada)
7-14-8 Roppongi, Minato-ku
Tokyo 106
Fax: 011-81-33-401-9321

Image from "Memory Scope" by
Peter & Skeeter DeMattia

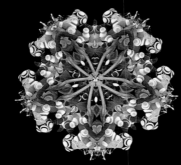

WHO'S WHO OF KALEIDOSCOPE ARTISTS

The designer of the kaleidoscope is as important to the connoisseur collector as the scope itself. A true kaleidoscope artist establishes his own individual mode or tone that renders his work almost as identifiable as his signature. This is not a comprehensive list of all the serious, excellent, and devoted Kaleidoscope makers, some of whom have been making scopes for over fifteen years, and others who have made literally thousands of them, Rather, it is limited to a selective honor roll of those who have achieved an "Oscar" or "Hall of Fame" status.

Various factors have been taken into consideration in compiling this list. These include the length of time an artist has been involved with scopes, and the volume of creative output. Many artists have developed one or two outstanding scopes, and stopped there. Still others make their own replicas of scopes that have already been developed. Although their work may be superb, there are other qualifications necessary for inclusion.

Each designer in the following Who's Who creates scopes based on his or her own ideas and imagination, and has initiated some original or unusual concept in their work. Not content to duplicate the work of others or to rest on the laurels of previous success, they continually expand creatively, improve techniques, and refine their craftsmanship. Over the years they have become a vital part of the kaleidoscope community by participating in the events that have ushered in the kaleidoscope renaissance.

Innovative designs, meticulous mirror systems, precision tooling, professional workmanship, and continuing experimentation distinguish these artists as outstanding exponents of excellence.

*Note: An * indicates the artist is no longer making kaleidoscopes. The date following each artist's company name is the year he or she started making scopes. The term "mixed" is used if he works with more than one medium.*

*An ** indicates the artist is deceased.*

"Let the Dreamers Wake the Nation" by Shantidevi and Sugito. Photo by Lisa Masson

"Fountain of Light" by Amy Hnatko. Photo by Laurie Bridgeforth

Image through "Meteor" by Leslie Martin & Sabina Diehr. Photo by George Erml

Bob and Grace Ade (Ade Enterprises)	1983	Glass
B. T. Ansley, IV	1992	Alabaster
Stephen Auger*	1975	Brass
Don Ballwey	1989	Glass (Egyptian motif)
Carolyn Bennett (C. Bennett Scopes)	1973	Acrylic
Henry Bergeson (Blackfoot Ventures)	1988	Wood
Debbie Brodel (See Rosenfeldt)		
Peggy Burnside (See Kittelson)		
Janice and Ray Chesnik	1980	Brass, wood, and glass
Tom Chouteau	1990	Wood (large and outdoor scopes)
R. Scott Cole	1982	Glass (teaches classes)
Carmen and Stephen Colley* (Gallocolley Glass)	1983	Glass
David L. Collier (Collier Products, Inc.)	1987	Wood
Robert Cook and Jocelyn Teh (Arcana Kaleidoscopes)-Australia	1989	Metal
Allen Crandell*	1990	Glass (Wheels)
John Culver	1979	Glass (Marbles)
Debra Davis	1991	Glass
Peter and Skeeter DeMattia (Originals by Skeeter)	1991	Mixed
Don Doak	1986	Glass
Luc and Sallie Durette (Secret Garden Kaleidoscopes)	1983	Mixed
Dennis and Diane Falconer* (Concept Center)	1986	Glass and wood
Marti Freund	1981	Glass and gourds
Steven Gray* (Gray & Gray Woodwrights)	1984	Wood
Stan Griffith* (And on the Eighth Day)	1988	Glass (marbles)
Ritama Haaga (Valhalla Studios)	1985	Glass
James Dana Hill	1987	Mixed
Amy Hnatko*	1986	Glass
Craig and Annie Huber (Galaxy Glass)	1983	Mixed
Wiley Jobe	Early 1990s	Wood
Doug and Dottie Johnson (Windseye)	1978	Glass and brass
David Kalish (Chromascopes)	1983	Mixed
Charles Karadimos	1980	Glass
Judith Karelitz**	1971	Acrylic (polarized light)
Peggy and Steve Kittelson (Woodland Glass)	1983	Glass
Randy and Shelley Knapp (Knapp Studios)	1989	Mixed
Sheryl Koch	1980	Mixed
Dean Krause*	1987	Mixed (jewelry and miniatures)

Jack Lazarowski and Tim Grannis* (Prism Designs)	1983	Brass and mirrors
Andrew and Robyn Leary (Scopes New Zealand)	1990s	Wood
Ron and Claudia Lee (Laughing Coyote)	1982	Mixed
Earl McNeil (Serendipity)	1985	Polarized light and wood
Bob McWilliam	1983	Wood and glass
Michael and Lisa Miron (The Kaleidoscope Works)	1990s	Mixed
Dorothea Marshall (Evans)*	1978	Mixed
Barbara Mitchell	1983	Mixed
Sherry Moser (The Moser Studio)	1985	Glass
Craig Musser** (Van Dyke, Ltd.)	1980	Mixed
Bill O'Connor	1980	Wood and brass
Ralph Olson (The Platte River Kaleidoscope Co.)	1990	Mixed
Carol and Tom Paretti (Workingwood)	1979	Wood
Adam Peiperl	1989	Polarized Light
Gordon and Analeise Redmond (Old World Glass)	1986	Glass
Michael and Stephanie Redmond (Mystic Illusion)	1994	Wood
Mark and Carole Reynolds (Kaleidovisions) (Acquired brother Peach's business in 1989)		Mixed
Peach Reynolds* (Kaleidoscopes by Peach)	1979	Mixed
Bob and Sue Rioux (The Sea Parrot)	1993	Glass
Debbie and David Rosenfeldt (Shipwrecked)	1991	Glass
Sue Ross (Jewelry Box Kaleidoscopes)	1983	Glass
Shantidevi*	1979	Glass
Will Smith (Minz Eye Studio)	1993	Acrylic
Peter Stephens*	1980	Mixed
Willie Stevenson* (Spirit Scopes)	1983	Metal
Glenn and Ben Straub (Wood You Believe)	1984	Wood
Massimo Strino (Imago Visual Art)	1994	Mixed
David Sugich (Ultimate Reflections)	1995	Glass
Dan Tarr	1989	Glass
Tom Thresher* (Tom Thresher Stoneworks)	1994	Alabaster and Corian®
Marc Tickle (On Reflection) England	1990	Glass
Erik and Kate Van Cort (Van Cort Instruments)	1982	Brass and wood
Corki Weeks	1983	Mixed
Ken and Dore Wilhoite	1995	Metal
Kay Winkler	1986	Glass
David York	1983	Glass

TIPS FOR CREATING YOUR OWN KALEIDOSCOPE

The most essential element needed for making a kaleidoscope is a love of the instrument itself. Then comes the added impetus of creativity. These all-important factors tend to be overlooked in the "how-to" books. But they are what make the difference between an exciting new achievement and just another replica.

For some unexplained reason, kaleidoscopes are a tremendous success only when the artist appreciates them for more than their monetary value. To some extent this is true of many objects; however, it is especially evident with kaleidoscopes. Maybe that can be attributed to the "spirit" behind (or within) each scope.

Another frequently overlooked factor of importance in creating your own kaleidoscope is an inquisitive and exploring disposition. Without exception, those artists who search on their own to find the necessary materials and sources for learning are the ones who make a name for themselves and whose work is recognized as distinctively original.

A questionnaire concerning the creative process was sent to a few highly respected artists. Their answers may suggest some helpful hints and good advice.

Question: How did you go about learning to make kaleidoscopes?

Janice Chesnik **Ray and I had to experiment, try things, and go on our own. There were no books or classes on the subject then. I shudder when I see one of our early scopes, but it is all we knew at the time.**

Sherry Moser **I spent hours in the library pouring over the *Thomas Registry* because I didn't even know what front-surface mirrors were. I also didn't know that any other mirror system existed except the equilateral three-mirror. I began to teach myself and explore possibilities. Later, I had the good fortune to meet other caring and sharing artists.**

Will Smith **Being naive to the fact that kaleidoscopes already existed in the market place as a beautiful art form, I blindly experimented on my own, using primitive resources until meeting kaleidoscope enthusiasts and artists willing to share their knowledge, for which I am most grateful.**

Charles Karadimos **Mostly by a focused trial-and-error approach, plus exploring, after starting with an article from the *Encyclopedia Britannica*.**

Sue Rioux **We experimented with mirror formations, construction techniques, and object case elements until we discovered what we were looking for. The innovation that flowed out of our early pieces can be mostly attributed to playing around with various materials.**

Question: What is your procedure for designing a scope?

Don Doak **I imagine it—then it takes only two or three days to actually build the first one. I see an image in my mind—and spend weeks or months figuring out how to do it.**

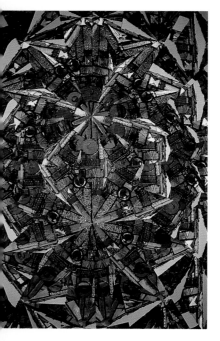

Four-mirror interior image by
Bob & Sue Rioux

Sherry Moser **I spend a lot of time visualizing a new piece in my head. However, it is only after I begin to make prototypes and see what problems occur in making this piece that it fully comes together. Most of my completed work is totally different from my original ideas.**

Charles Karadimos **First I design the mirror system since I feel that is the most important part. Then for the rest, sketching, sketching, and more sketching is a good way to work out problems before actually starting construction.**

Sue & Bob Rioux **We discuss ideas and brainstorm new directions. None of our pieces are designed on paper. We try to push beyond the realm of current creation to something unique. Then we go straight from conception to a three-dimensional vision that we can turn and manipulate. Little is changed from this mental picture when the actual piece is constructed.**

Janice Chesnik **Keeping it simple is the key for us. Ray and I will sit at the kitchen table and sketch new shapes and designs, all the while asking, "Is it workable, does it have class, is it beautiful inside, and will others want it?" Sometimes we study interior design books and magazines for inspiration.**

Question: What is the one piece of advice you would give prospective designers?

Janice Chesnik **Be original above all else! Love what you are doing, and be the best you can be by being open to learning new things, changing and evolving.**

Sue Rioux **Make sure the design comes from within. Observe others' work as inspiration and then let your own ideas develop into a work all your own.**

Will Smith **Set high standards—the rest will follow.**

Sherry Moser **Listen to advice, but don't create pieces just because you think that is what will sell.**

Charles Karadimos **Don't let the frustrations of progress hold you back from trying again. Be encouraged by what you have accomplished with each step toward your goal. Learn from your previous experiences and be patient. Just keep on keeping on.**

Dean Krause **When you put love into a project, it gets noticed. The world is alive with creativity; get in touch with it and let it permeate your whole life. Do not partition it off to something you do in your spare time.**

Don Doak **Learn how to cut, lap, and chamfer, and assemble your mirrors so they are perfect. Then and only then apply your own talents and skills to the exterior. Next, look at what everyone else is doing. Then turn your back on their work and go in a direction no one has ever been before. Only then will you be creative.**

Interior image by Charles Karadimos

Don Doak does more than give advice on learning to cut mirrors. He has developed a way to cut, lap, chamfer, lay out angles, and clean mirrors that can be learned by anyone. This information is available on a two hour "how-to" video (see bibliography). He has also developed and patented a magnetic glass cutter that is so simple even a child can cut straight mirrors within one ten-thousandth of an inch. Using his methods and the magnetic cutter, anyone

Clockwise from Right:
Fused flower scopes by Peggy &
Steve Kittelson. Handpainted iris
scope, Kay Winkler. Parlor wheel
scope, Carmen & Stephen Colley.
White dichroic handheld scope,
Kittelsons. Photo by John Woodin

Wheel scope by Allen Crandell.
Photo by Laurie Bridgeforth

"Whirlwind" by Michael &
Stephanie Redmond. Photo by
Donna Mcwilliam

"Parlor Scope Series II," by Bob
McWilliam

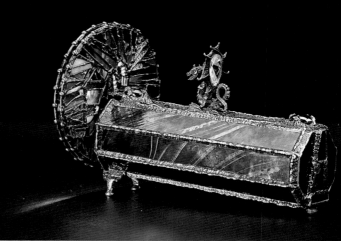

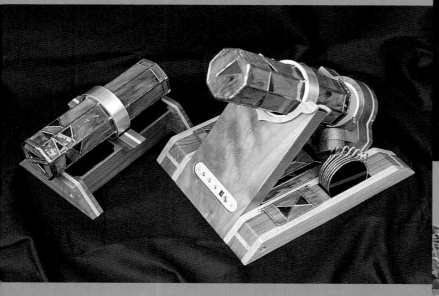

Clockwise from Left:
"Party at Level Sea and Bring Your Own Bubbles," carousel scope by Sue Ross

Parlor ball-bearing scope by Jerry Beall in fitted mahogany box. Photo by Judith Beall

Image from "Aurora" by the Durettes

Christmas scopes by the Durettes

can cut and prepare a flawless set of mirrors capable of creating a perfect illusion with none of the distractions caused by cracked, flaked, splintered, dirty, or poorly cut mirrors. And no matter how beautiful the objects to be viewed, if the mirrors are wrong, the image will be faulty.

Those who ask, "After the mirrors are cut, then what?" would do well to study Brewster's patent on page 132. The casual reader usually skims over this document, if not overlooking it entirely. But for anyone seriously interested in learning the technical procedure for making a kaleidoscope, there is no better or more accurate source than the inventor's original specifications. The patent, together with a perusal of the mirror systems on page 68, and the sources for key materials listed at the end of this appendix, is tantamount to a course in "Kaleidoscopes 101." The rest is up to each individual's own ideas, imagination, and creativity. Happy scoping!

SOURCES FOR KALEIDOSCOPE MATERIALS

Lenses
Glass
La Croix
P.O. Box 2556, Batesville, AR
(501) 698-1881

Plastic
JP Manufacturing Inc.
13 Lovely St. Southbridge, MA 01550
(508) 764-2538
Fax: (508) 765-1312

Brass Tubing
Automatic Tubing Corporation
888 Lorimer St., Brooklyn, NY 11222
(718) 383-0100

Front-Surface Mirror
Dean Franssell
8275 Country Rd 116, Hamel, MN 55340
(612) 420-4810

Stained Glass
D & L Stained Glass Supply, Inc.
(800) 525-0940
Fax: (303) 442-3429

Ed Hoy's International
1020 Frontenac, Naperville, IL 60565
(630) 355-7557

OR
Check your local stained glass retailers

Video
A complete video on how to prepare front-surface mirrors by Don Doak is available from:
Delphi Stained Glass
3380 E. Jolly Rd., Lansing, MI 48910
(800) 248-2048

Opposite: Chart of Principles and Construction of the Kaleidoscope from an early encyclopedia.
Courtesy of Bill Carroll

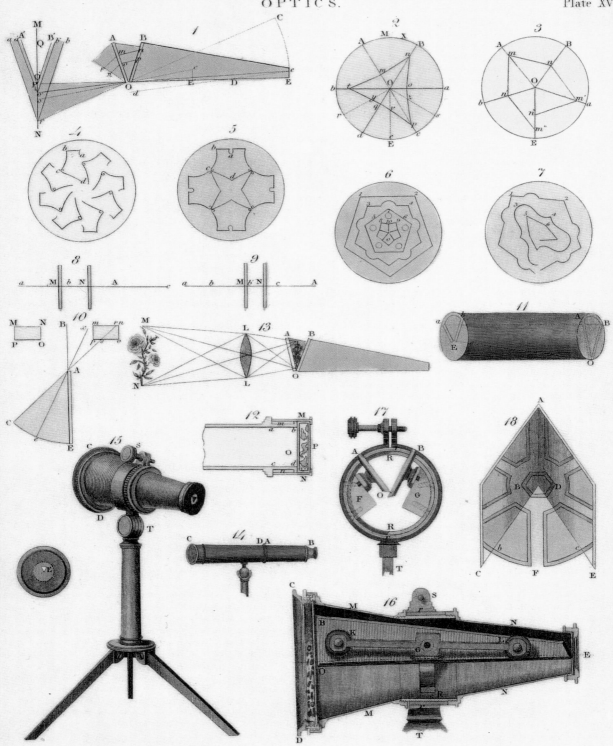

Principles and Construction of the Kaleidoscope.

Engraved for the Encyclopædia Londinensis 1820

T. Bass sc

BREWSTER AND BUSH PATENTS

BREWSTER PATENT

A.D.1817   No 4136
Kaleidoscopes

BREWSTER'S SPECIFICATION

TO ALL WHOM THESE PRESENTS SHALL COME, I, David Brewster, of Edinburgh, Doctor of Laws, send greeting.

WHEREAS His present most Excellent Majesty King George the Third did by His Royal Letters Patent under the Great Seal of the United Kingdom of Great Britain and Ireland, bearing date at Westminster, the Tenth day of July, in the fifty-seventh year of His reign, give and grant unto me, the said David Brewster, my executors, administrators, and assigns, His especial full power, sole privilege and authority, that I, the said David Brewster, my executors, administrators, and assigns, during the term of years therein expressed, should and lawfully might make, use, exercise, and vend my NEW OPTICAL INSTRUMENT CALLED THE KALEIDOSCOPE FOR EXHIBITING AND TREATING BEAUTIFUL FORMS AND PATTERNS, OR GREAT USE IN ALL THE ORNAMENTAL ARTS within England, Wales, and the Town of Berwick-upon-Tweed, in such manner as to me, the said David Brewster, my executors, administrators, and designs should in our discretion seem meet; in which said Letters Patent is certified a proviso that if I, the said David Brewster, should not particularly describe and ascertain the nature of my said Invention, and in what manner the same is to be performed, by an instrument in writing under my hand and seal, and cause the same to be inrolled in His Majesty's High Court of Chancery within two calendar months next and immediately after the date of the said Letters Patent, that then the said Letters Patent, and all liberties and advantages whatsoever thereby granted, should utterly cease, determine, and become void, as in and by the said recited Letters Patent, relation being there unto had, may more fully and at large appear.

The kaleidoscope (from χαωλοζ, beautiful; ειδοζ, a form; and σχοπεω, to see) is an instrument for creating and exhibiting an infinite variety of beautiful forms, and is constructed in such a manner as either to please the eye by an ever-varying succession of splendid tints and symmetrical forms, or to enable the observer to render permanent such as may appear most appropriate for any of the numerous branches of the ornamental arts. This instrument in its most common form consists of two reflecting surfaces inclined to each other at any angle, but more properly at an angle which is an aliquot part of 360°. The reflecting surfaces may be two plates of glass plain or quicksilvered, or two metallic surfaces, or the two inner surfaces of a solid prism of glass or rock chrystal, from which the light suffers total reflection. The plates should vary in length according to the focal distance of the eye; 5, 6, 7, 8, 9, and 10 inches will in general be most convenient; or they may be made only 1, 2, 3, or 4 inches long, provided distinct vision is obtained at one end by placing at the other end an eye glass whose focal length is equal to the length of the reflecting planes. The inclination of the reflectors that is in general most pleasing is 18°, 20°, or 22 $^1/_2$°, or the 20th, 18th, and 16th part of a circle; but the planes may be set at any required angle either by a metallic, a paper, or cloth joint, or any other simple contrivance. When the two planes are put together with their straightest and smoothest edges in contact, they will have form shewn in Figure 1, where A, B, C, is the aperture or angle formed by the plates. In

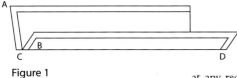

Figure 1

this Figure the plates are rectangular, but it may often be more convenient to give them the triangular form shewn at M, Fig. 2, or N, Fig. 3.

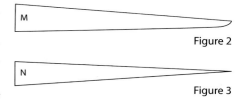

Figure 2

Figure 3

When the instrument is thus constructed, it may be either covered up with paper or leather or placed in a cylindrical or any other tube, so that the aperture A, B, C may be left completely open, and also a small aperture at the angular point D. If the eye is now placed at D, and looks thro' the aperture A, B, C, it will perceive a brilliant circle of light, divided into as many sectors as the number of times that the angle of the reflector is contained in 360°. If this angle is 18° the number of sectors will be 20; and whatever be the form of the aperture A, B, C, the luminous space seen thro' the instrument will be a figure produced by the arrangement of 20 of these apertures round C as a centre, in consequence of the successive reflexions between the polished surfaces. Hence, it follows, that if any object, however ugly or irregular in itself, is placed before the aperture A, B, C, the part of it that can be seen through the aperture will be seen also in every sector, and every image of the object will be seen also in every sector, and every image of the object will coalesce into a form mathematically symmetrical and highly pleasing to the eye. If the object is put in motion, the combination of images will likewise be put in motion, and new forms, perfectly different but equally symmetrical, will successively present themselves, sometimes vanishing in the centre, sometimes emerging from it, and sometimes playing around in double and opposite oscillations. When the object is tinged with different colours, the most beautiful tints are developed in succession, and the whole figure delights the eye by the perfection of its forms and the brilliancy of its colouring. The motion of the object may be affected either by the hand or by a simple piece of mechanism, or the same effect may be produced by the motion of the instrument over the object or round its own axis. In the form of the kaleidoscope now described the object should be held close to the aperture A, B, C, and the eye should be placed as nearly as possible in the line C, D, for the figure loses its symmetry in proportion as the object recedes from A, B, C, and as the eye rises above D. The instrument is therefore limited in its present form to the use of objects which can be held close to the aperture. In order to remove the limitation, the tube which contains the reflectors should slide in another tube of nearly the same length, and having a convex lens at its further extremity; the focal length of the lens should be always less than its greatest distance from the aperture A, B, C. In general it should be about $^1/_3$ or $^1/_4$ of that distance, but it will be adviseable to have two or even three lenses of different focal lengths to fit into the end of the outer tube, and to be used as circumstance may require, or a variation of focal length may be produced by the separation or approach of two lenses. When the instrument is thus fitted up it may be applied to objects at all distances, and these objects, whose images are formed in an inverted position at the aperture A, B, C, may be introduced into the symmetrical picture in the very same manner as if they were brought close to the instrument. Hence, we can introduce trees, flowers, statues, and living animals, and any object which is too large to be comprehended by the aperture A, B, C, may be removed to such a distance that its image is sufficiently reduced. The kaleidoscope is also constructed with three or more reflecting planes, which may be arranged in various ways. The tints placed before the aperture may be the complementary colors produced by transmitting polarised light thro' regularly chrystallized bodies or pieces of glass that have received the polarising structure. The partial polarisation of the light by successive relfexions occasions a partial analysis of the transmitted light; but in order to develop the tints with brilliancy, the analysis of the light must procede its admission into the aperture. Instead of looking thro' the extremity D of the tube, the effects which have been described may be exhibited to many persons at once, upon the principle of the solar microscope or magic lanthorn, and in this way, or by the application of the camera lucida, the figures may be accurately delineated. It would be an endless task to point out the various purposes in the ornamental arts to which the kaleidoscope is applicable. It may be sufficient to state, that it will be of great use for architects, ornamental painters, plasterers, jewelers, carvers and gliders, cabinet makers, wire workers, bookbinders, calico printers, carpet manufacturers, manufacturers of pottery, and every other profession in which ornamental patterns are required. The painter may introduce the very colours which he is to use; the jeweler, the jewels which he is to arrange; and in general, the artist may apply to the instrument the materials which he is to embody, and thus form the most correct opinion of their effect when combined into an ornamental pattern.

When the instrument is thus applied, an infinity of patterns are created, and the artist can select such as he considers most suitable to his work. When a knowledge of the nature and powers of the instrument has been acquired by a little practice, he will be able to give any character to the pattern that he chooses, and he may even create a series of different patterns, all rising out of one another and returning by similar gradations to the first pattern of the series. In all these cases the pattern is perfectly symmetrical round a centre, or all the images of the aperture A, B, C, are exactly alike; but this symmetry may be altered, for after the pattern is drawn it may be reduced into a square, a triangular, an elliptical, or any other form that we please. The instrument will give annular patterns by keeping the reflectors separate as at A, B, Fig. 4, and it will give rectilineal ones by placing the reflectors parallel to each other, as in Fig. 5. The kaleidoscope is also proposed as an instrument of amusement to please the eye by the creation and exhibition of beautiful forms in the same manner as the ear is delighted by the combination of musical sounds. When Custillon proposed the construction of an ocular harpsichord, he was mistaken in supposing that any combination of harmonic colors could afford the pleasure to the person who viewed them, for it is only when these colours are connected with regular and beautiful forms that the eye is gratified by the combination. The kaleidoscope, therefore, seems to realise the idea of an ocular harpsichord.

In witness whereof, I, the said David Brewster, have hereunto set my hand and seal, this Twenty-seventh day of August, in the year of our Lord One thousand eight hundred and seventeen.

DAVID (L.S.) BREWSTER
Signed and sealed by the within-named
David Brewster (being first duly stamped) in the presence of us,
ARCHD MONTGOMERY, Witness, residing at Wherin, Parish of Newlands, and County of Peebles.
ROBT MONTGOMERY, Of Lincoln's Inn, Barrister at Law.

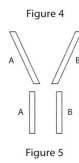

Figure 4

Figure 5

BUSH PATENT

UNITED STATES PATENT OFFICE

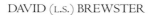

CHARLES G. BUSH, OF BOSTON, MASSACHUSETTS, ASSIGNOR TO HIMSELF AND JOHN W. HOARD. IMPROVEMENT IN KALEIDOSCOPES.

Specification forming part of Letters Patent No. 143, 271, dated September 30, 1873; reissue No. 5, 649, dated November 11, 1973; application filed October 30, 1873.

To all whom it may concern:

Be it known that I, CHARLES G. BUSH, of Boston, in the county of Suffolk and State of Massachusetts, have invented a new and useful Improved Object for the Object-Box of Kaleidoscopes; ...

In the rotation of the object-box, my compound tube, like any other object therein, is caused by gravity to fall into different positions.

A hollow glass object with two immiscible liquids and an air-bubble, contained therein is shown in Figs. 2 and 3, in which b is the vessel hermetically sealed, c and cI the two immiscible liquids, and d the air-bubble, the whole resembling a diminutive glass spirit-level.

I would remark that a glass tube, containing a single liquid and an air-bubble, the ends of the tube being closed by cement or plugging, is an object heretofore used by me, and not claimed in this application; and in carrying out my invention, in regard to the contents of the tube, I employ either two or more liquids of different densities or character, or a liquid with a solid or solids. I thus obtain two liquids or objects of different colors within the same vessel or tube, and which, by their relative movements within such tube, product new and pleasing effects.

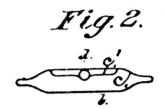

What I claim, therefore, as new in objects for the object-box of kaleidoscopes, is as follows:

1. In combination with a kaleidoscope-box, a glass tube or vessel for containing one or more objects, said tube or vessel being closed hermetically without the use of cement or plugging.

2. In combination with a kaleidoscope-box, an object, consisting of a glass tube or vessel containing liquid, and closed hermetically by the fusing of the glass without the aid of cement or plugging.

3. An object for kaleidoscopes, consisting of a glass tube or vessel containing two or more immiscible liquids, or one or more liquids and one or more solids.

CHARLES G. BUSH.

IMPROVEMENT IN OBJECT-BOXES FOR KALEIDOSCOPES

Specification Forming Part Of Letters Patent No. 151,006, Dated May 19, 1874; Application Filed March 20, 1874.
Be it known that I, CHAS. G. BUSH, of Boston, Massachusetts, have invented an Improvement in Object-Boxes for Kaleidoscopes, of which the following is a specification:

My invention consists in making the object-box of a kaleidoscope with an opening, and a cover for the same, for the ready introduction into or removal of the objects from the box, thus avoiding the necessity, as the boxes have been heretofore constructed, of taking the whole apparatus apart, and removing one of the glasses of the box, and then putting the parts together again.

I claim—

A kaleidoscope object-box, provided with an opening and movable cover therefor, substantially as and for the purpose set forth.

CHARLES G. BUSH.

IMPROVEMENT IN KALEIDOSCOPES

Specification forming part of Letters Patent No. 151,005, dated May 19, 1874; application filed December 20, 1873.
To all whom it may concern:
Be it known that I, CHAS. G. BUSH, of Boston, Massachusetts, have invented Improvements in Kaleidoscopes, of which the following is a specification:

My present invention consists in combining, with a rotating object-box, a means between the eye and object-box, for illuminating the objects, so that opaque objects, equally as well as transparent

ones, may be employed, and their colors fully displayed. It further consists in uniting in the same instrument the requisites for displaying properly the true colors both of opaque and translucent objects; in other words, merging, virtually, the two characters of instruments into one. It further consists in combining, with a kaleidoscope having a revolving object-box, a variegated colored cardboard or reflector, to be hung behind the instrument upon a stationery support, so that a background of any desired tint or color may be brought at will behind the object-glass, and thus give such background for the figure or design presented to the eye.

I claim—

1. The combination, in a kaleidoscope for opaque objects, of an independent revolving object-box, supported in near proximity to the objective end of the prism, and a transparent tube surrounding the objective end of the prism, and also serving as the support of said revolving box.

2. The combination, with a kaleidoscope for opaque objects, as described, of an independent revolving object-box, whose ends are both of glass, either perfectly plain, or the outer one ground and the inner one clear, for use wither with the transparent or opaque objects.

3. In combination with a kaleidoscope, the parti-colored reflecting card-board, adjustable, by rotation, to afford a series of backgrounds of any desired color, substantially as shown and described.

CHARLES G. BUSH.

IMPROVEMENT IN KALEIDOSCOPE-STANDS

Specification forming part of Letters Patent No. 156,875, dated November 17, 1874; application filed May 22, 1874.
To all whom it may concern:

Be it known that I, CHAS G. BUSH, of Boston, State of Massachusetts, have invented an Improvement in Stands for Parlor-Kaleidoscopes, &c., of which the following is a specification:

My improvement relates to the mode of constructing the stand and its legs, used for supporting a parlor-kaleidoscope and for similar purposes, the object being to facilitate the packing them in a small compact compass for transportation or storing away, and yet to readily put the same together firmly for use without the use of glue, nails, rivets, or any fastening device.

Heretofore kaleidoscope-stands for parlor use have been made with the standard or post secured or screwed into a solid block or base, which needed to be of considerable diameter, and was of thick expensive wood.

I claim—

The stand constructed with the cross-cuts in the post, and with the central cross-cuts in the cross-pieces which compose the legs or base, the whole being fitted and adapted to be united and held together by pressure and frictional contact only, and to be instantly taken apart, in the manner and for the purpose shown and described.

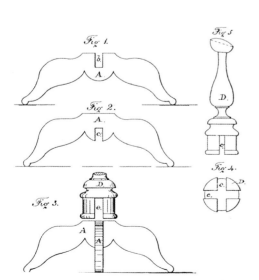

CHARLES G. BUSH.

In the last year or two, America has gone bonkers for the Internet. There's hardly a product or service left that doesn't urge you to visit a home page or send comments via e-mail.

At the recent Brewster Convention, as we heard scope people expressing interest in the Internet, it occurred to us that kaleidoscope viewing has a kinship with the Net. Both are full of color and fun, both are controlled by the viewer.

There are thousands of references on the Internet under kaleidoscope. Most of them use the word as a metaphor for things unrelated to mirrors and object chambers. A few offer eye-catching kaleidoscopic images, and a handful provide information for kaleidoscope collectors.

For those who are interested in the Internet but hesitate to enter strange territory—quit worrying. Using the Internet requires far less skill than driving a car. Once you're set up, it's no harder than accessing your bank account using an ATM (Automatic Teller Machine).

Let's say you own a computer and want to see what's on the Internet. All you need is a modem for your computer, a service provider to connect you with the Internet, and some software to get started.

A **modem** is communications hardware that transfers data between your computer and the Internet over a phone line. Modems are rated by the speed at which they send and receive data (baud rate). The higher the number, the faster the service.

A **service provider** is the switchboard between your computer/modem and the Internet. Your best choice is a service provider whose access phone number is in your Flat Rate Service calling area. Look for a company offering unlimited time on the Internet. Your service provider usually provides the software you'll need to access the wonderful world of the Internet.

That's all there is to it. Once you're cruising the Internet you'll find it's easy to look things up by subject. You'll find your own way, following prompts, taking little joy rides, poking into this doorway, peering in that window, running around the block, getting lost in strange neighborhoods but always ending up safely at home.

You'll find, as we did, that the Internet is an amazing grab-bag of fun and useful stuff. You can rent a car, play games, download maps for the trip you're planning, browse the world's web sites, chat with other users, and scroll

*Reprinted courtesy of Shel and Jan Haber, Hand of the Craftsman, Nyack, NY

catalogs of things to buy from racing gear to vitamins. You can access libraries here and abroad, and read electronic magazines on everything from gardening to politics, or communicate with people who share your interests anywhere in the world—all for the cost of a local phone call.

For you newbies: Don't be intimidated by these mile-long site addresses. They're no more complex than the familiar name, address, city, state, and zip code but they look weird because of the unfamiliar mix of small letters and symbols.

Like the Postal Service, the Internet loses mis-addressed letters. Unlike the Post Office, the Inernet forgives no errors. An envelope with a misplaced comma probably won't end up in Post Office limbo, but on the Internet, dealing with the ultra-literal cyberbrain behind your computer, it's all or nothing, so enter those addresses with precision.

Following are some sites to behold—outstanding views for lovers of kaleidoscopes.

ON-LINE SHOPPING

A Mano Galleries/Martin & Ana Leyland
New Hope and Lambertville, PA
On-line store; photos of several popular scopes
http://www.amanogalleries.com/index.html

Davlins/Dave & Linda Looney
Minneapolis, Roseville, Edina, MN
On-line store with data about history and how scopes are made
http://www.kaliedo.com/home.htm

Hand of the Craftsman/Shel & Jan Haber
Nyack, NY
On-line store; kaleidoscope history; how scopes work; on-line collector's magazine
http://www.kaleidoscopesUSA.com

Kaleidoscope World/Karl & Jean Schilling
Red Wing, MN
On-line store; photos of kaleidoscopes
http://www.viawebcom/scopes/

Eileen Kremen Gallery/Eileen Kremen
Fullerton, CA
On-line store; photos of kaleidoscopes and other art
http://www.members@aol.com/ekremen

Stardust Gallery/David Meelheim
Mclean, VA
http://www.stardustgallery.com

Veranda/Jan & Bobby Boal
Senoia, GA
http://www.kaleidoscopeshop.com

LISTS, INFORMATION & MISCELLANEOUS

Kaleidoscope Heaven/Brett Bensley
Information about kaleidoscopes, kaleidoscope dealers, artists, and events. Pictures of scopes and links to well-known and lesser-known scope makers
http://www.kaleidoscopeheaven.org/

Zipper Base
A squirrely collection of photos and quotations with gorgeous scope images.
http://www.zenzero.com/zipper04.html

ARTISTS' ON-LINE CATALOGS

Originals by Skeeter/Peter & Skeeter DeMattia
http://www.members.tripod.com/˜Skeeter_DeMattia/index.html

Van Cort Instruments/Kate & Eric Van Cort
http://www.vancort.com

Windseye Kaleidoscopes/Doug & Dottie Johnson
http://www.cei.net/˜windseye

KALEIDO-GLOSSARY

Ampule - small, sealed glass container.

Cell - Same as object case or chamber.

Decahedron - A solid figure with ten faces.

Dichroic - Glass that reflects different colors depending on the angle at which the light hits it. (Dichroic glass is created by a vacuum process that deposits multiple layers of metals onto the surface of glass. The glass manipulates light by transmitting one color through the glass while a second color is reflected from the surface; hence the name dichroic.)

Disc - Object case.

Dodecahedron - A solid figure with twelve faces.

First-surface mirror - Mirror in which reflecting metal is on the front surface of the glass, rather than behind the rear surface as in a conventional mirror.

Flamework - See Lampworking.

Front-surface mirror - Same as first-surface mirror.

Fused glass - Colored pieces of glass joined together by heating in a kiln.

Hedron - A combining form used in the names of geometrical solid figures with the number of faces specified by the initial element.

Icosahedron - A solid figure with twenty faces.

Lampworking - A process using a specially designed torch or lamp to heat glass rods for sculpting, blowing, or beadmaking.

Latticinio - Embedded threads of swirling white and colored glass.

Lens - A piece of glass or other transparent substance with two opposing curved surfaces, or one plane surface and one curved surface.

Mandala - A circular design containing concentric geometric forms, symbolizing wholeness.

Millefiori - Many cross-section slices of multicolored glass in floral-like designs.

Object case - Container at end of scope holding objects to be viewed.

Polarized Light - Light that vibrates in one plane only (in contrast to ordinary light, which vibrates in all directions).

Polyhedron - A solid figure with many faces.

Shards - Slivers of glass.

Teleidoscope - (from the Greek: distant-form-viewing) A kaleidoscope in which the object case is a lens, or one having no object case at all. Whatever it is pointed toward is reflected again and again in kaleidoscopic patterns.

BIBLIOGRAPHY

Arguelles, Jose and Miriam. *Mandala*, Shambala, Colorado, 1972.

Baker, Cozy. *Kaleidorama*, Beechcliff Books, Bethesda, MD, 1990.

Baker, Cozy. *Kaleidoscope Renaissance*, Beechcliff Books, Bethesda, MD, 1993.

Baker, Cozy. *Through the Kaleidoscope. . . And Beyond*, Beechcliff Books, Bethesda, MD, 1987.

Boswell, Thom. *The Kaleidoscope Book :A Spectrum of Spectacular Scopes to Make*, Sterling/Lark Books, NY, 1992.

Brewster, Sir David. *A Treatise on the Kaleidoscope* (Edinburgh: Archibald Constable & Co., 1819).

Brewster, Sir David. *The Kaleidoscope—Its History, Theory, and Construction with its Application to the Fine and Useful Arts*, second, enlarged edition (London: John Murray, 1858).

The Brewster Society (an organization for kaleidoscope artists, collectors and enthusiasts) P.O. Box 1073, Bethesda, Maryland 20817; 301-365-1855; 301-365-2284 (fax).

The Brewster Society *News Scope*, a quarterly newsletter published by the Brewster Society.

Cornall, Judith. *Mandala: Luminous Symbols for Healing*, Theosophical Publishing House, Wheaton, IL, 1994.

"Martyr of Science," Sir David Brewster, 1781-1868, edited by A.D. Morrison– Low and J.R.R. Christie, Royal Scottish Museum Studies, Edinburgh, Scotland, 1984. Proceedings of a Bicentenary Symposium held Nov. 21, 1981.

Middleman, Ruth H. and Gary B. Rhodes.*Competent Supervision: Making Imaginative Judgments*, Prentice-Hall, Englewood Cliffs, NJ, 1985.

Nadelstern, Paula. *Kaleidoscopes & Quilts*, C&T Publishing, Concord, CA, 1996.

Newlin, Gary. *Simple Kaleidoscopes*, Sterling/Lark Books, NY 1995.

Smith, Graham. *Disciples of Light, Photographs in the Brewster Album*, The J. Paul Getty Museum, Los Angeles, 1990.

Yoder, Walter D. *Kaleidoscopes, The Art of Mirrored Magic [an overview of the historical development, patent literature, design techniques (including computer), and marketing of kaleidoscopes]*, from the author, 8417 Capuliin NE, Albuquerque, NM, 1988 (rev. 1998).

INDEX

ABOUT THE AUTHOR

Cozy Baker is internationally recognized as the First Lady of Kaleidoscopes because of the many firsts she has introduced. After writing the first book on the subject, she curated the nation's first kaleidoscope exhibition, and formed the world's first organization for kaleidoscope enthusiasts. As founding president of the Brewster Society (in honor of Sir David Brewster, the scope's inventor), Baker functions as a kaleidoscope clearinghouse, museum, and network for its members. She devotes full time to writing, consulting, collecting, and sharing with others the joys of her favorite art form. She resides in Bethesda, Maryland, delighting in the proximity of her two married children, and four grandchildren.

Other titles by Cozy Baker include *A Cozy Getaway*, *Holiday Frame of Mind*, *Love Beyond Life*, *Through the Kaelsidoscope...and Beyond*, *Kaleidoscope Renaissance*, and *Kaleidoscopia* (a calendar for the last five years of the 1990s).

Photo by Lisa Masson

IN APPRECIATION

I want to express heartfelt thanks to my daughter, Barbi Richardson, who helped immensely with the editing and preparation of each chapter of this book. And sincere gratitude goes to my friend Linda Joy, who contributed in so many helpful ways in whatever capacity was needed.

A special thank you also to each artist, collector, and shop owner who provided a photograph or shared an idea to help complete this pictorial history of the wonderful world of kaleidoscopes.

Designed by David Fulkerson and executed by Joe Kennard

The kaleidoscope opens a window

to glance inside your wish . . .

or escape into your dream

OTHER FINE BOOKS FROM C&T PUBLISHING

An Amish Adventure: 2nd Edition, Roberta Horton

Anatomy of a Doll: The Fabric Sculptor's Handbook,
  Susanna Oroyan

Appliqué 12 Easy Ways! Elly Sienkiewicz

Art & Inspirations: Ruth B. McDowell, Ruth B. McDowell

The Art of Silk Ribbon Embroidery, Judith Baker Montano

The Artful Ribbon, Candace Kling

Baltimore Beauties and Beyond (Volume I), Elly Sienkiewicz

Basic Seminole Patchwork, Cheryl Greider Bradkin

Beyond the Horizon: Small Landscape Appliqué, Valerie Hearder

Buttonhole Stitch Appliqué, Jean Wells

A Colorful Book, Yvonne Porcella

Colors Changing Hue, Yvonne Porcella

Crazy Quilt Handbook, Judith Montano

Crazy Quilt Odyssey, Judith Montano

Crazy with Cotton, Diana Leone

Curves in Motion: Quilt Designs & Techniques, Judy B. Dales

Deidre Scherer: Work in Fabric & Thread, Deidre Scherer

Dimensional Appliqué: Baskets, Blooms & Baltimore Borders,
  Elly Sienkiewicz

Easy Pieces: Creative Color Play with Two Simple Blocks,
  Margaret Miller

*Elegant Stitches: An Illustrated Stitch Guide & Source Book of
  Inspiration*, Judith Baker Montano

Enduring Grace: Quilts from the Shelburne Museum Collection,
  Celia Y. Oliver

Everything Flowers: Quilts from the Garden,
  Jean and Valori Wells

The Fabric Makes the Quilt, Roberta Horton

Faces & Places: Images in Appliqué, Charlotte Warr Andersen

Fantastic Figures: Ideas & Techniques Using the New Clays,
  Susanna Oroyan

Focus on Features: Life-like Portrayals in Appliqué,
  Charlotte Warr Andersen

Forever Yours, Wedding Quilts, Clothing & Keepsakes,
  Amy Barickman

Fractured Landscape Quilts, Katie Pasquini Masopust

Free Stuff for Quilters on the Internet,
  Judy Heim and Gloria Hansen

*From Fiber to Fabric: The Essential Guide to Quiltmaking
  Textiles*, Harriet Hargrave

*Hand Quilting with Alex Anderson: Six Projects for Hand
  Quilters*, Alex Anderson

Heirloom Machine Quilting, Third Edition, Harriet Hargrave

Imagery on Fabric, Second Edition, Jean Ray Laury

Impressionist Palette, Gai Perry

Impressionist Quilts, Gai Perry

Jacobean Rhapsodies: Composing with 28 Appliqué Designs,
  Pat Campbell and Mimi Ayars

Judith B. Montano: Art & Inspirations, Judith B. Montano

Kaleidoscopes & Quilts, Paula Nadelstern

Mariner's Compass Quilts, New Directions, Judy Mathieson

Mastering Machine Appliqué, Harriet Hargrave

Michael James: Art & Inspirations, Michael James

The New Sampler Quilt, Diana Leone

On the Surface: Thread Embellishment & Fabric Manipulation,
  Wendy Hill

Papercuts and Plenty, Vol. III of Baltimore Beauties and Beyond,
  Elly Sienkiewicz

Patchwork Persuasion: Fascinating Quilts from Traditional Designs,
  Joen Wolfrom

Patchwork Quilts Made Easy, Jean Wells (co-published
  with Rodale Press, Inc.)

Pattern Play, Doreen Speckmann

Pieced Clothing Variations, Yvonne Porcella

Pieces of an American Quilt, Patty McCormick

Piecing: Expanding the Basics, Ruth B. McDowell

Plaids & Stripes: The Use of Directional Fabrics in Quilts,
  Roberta Horton

Quilts for Fabric Lovers, Alex Anderson

Quilts from the Civil War: Nine Projects, Historical Notes,
  Diary Entries, Barbara Brackman

Quilts, Quilts, and More Quilts!
  Diana McClun and Laura Nownes

Recollections, Judith Baker Montano

RIVA: If Ya Wanna Look Good Honey, Your Feet Gotta Hurt. . .,
  Ruth Reynolds

Say It with Quilts, Diana McClun and Laura Nownes

Scrap Quilts: The Art of Making Do, Roberta Horton

Simply Stars: Quilts that Sparkle, Alex Anderson

Six Color World: Color, Cloth, Quilts & Wearables,
  Yvonne Porcella

Small Scale Quiltmaking: Precision, Proportion, and Detail,
  Sally Collins

Soft-Edge Piecing, Jinny Beyer

*Start Quilting with Alex Anderson: Six Projects for First-Time
  Quilters*, Alex Anderson

Stripes in Quilts, Mary Mashuta

Tradition with a Twist: Variations on Your Favorite Quilts,
  Blanche Young and Dalene Young Stone

Trapunto by Machine, Hari Walner

The Visual Dance: Creating Spectacular Quilts, Joen Wolfrom

Wildflowers: Designs for Appliqué & Quilting,
  Carol Armstrong

Willowood: Further Adventures in Buttonhole Stitch Appliqué,
  Jean Wells

Yvonne Porcella: Art & Inspirations, Yvonne Porcella

For more information write for a free catalog:

C&T Publishing, Inc.
P.O. Box 1456
Lafayette, CA 94549
(800) 284-1114
http://www.ctpub.com
e-mail: ctinfo@ctpub.com

For quilting supplies:

Cotton Patch Mail Order
3405 Hall Lane, Dept. CTB
Lafayette, CA 94549
e-mail: cottonpa@aol.com
(800) 835-4418
(925) 283-7883